Criminal Justice Career Opportunities

in Ohio

Katherine A. Steinbeck

Professor & Program Director
Criminal Justice
Lakeland Community College
Kirtland, Ohio

Daniel F. Ponstingle

Professor & Program Director, Retired
Lorain County Community College
Elyria, Ohio

KENDALL/HUNT PUBLISHING COMPANY
4050 Westmark Drive   Dubuque, Iowa 52002

To our students and prospective criminal justice practitioners, with special thanks to Carole and Lisa for their unwavering support.

CONTENTS

SECTION III: CORRECTIONS CAREERS

CHAPTER 6: COVERING CORRECTIONS CAREERS

CHAPTER 7: PRIVATIZATION OF CORRECTIONS

PREFACE

WHY SHOULD YOU USE THIS WORKBOOK?

Abraham Lincoln said it best: "People who like this sort of thing will find this the sort of thing they like."

WHY IS THIS CAREER BOOK DIFFERENT?

With over 50 years combined experience in teaching community college-based, criminal justice students, we are certain of three truths:

- Prospective criminal justice employees are practical people with very little non-dedicated "free" time. Therefore, this is a goal-oriented workbook, designed to help the prospective employee consider and apply career-related topics and tasks to *his/her* own life, rather than have the *authors* discuss career opportunities and processes in an abstract, generic and non-interactive format.

- While there are nationally-based, criminal justice-related opportunities and processes, Ohio is still unique. (If it weren't, the nation would not be subdivided into separate states!) Therefore, it is more practical for an Ohio resident to read an Ohio-based career employment text than a generic, one-text-meets-all needs. (However, to enhance the reader's career exploration, we have included a comprehensive overview of federal-level, criminal justice employment opportunities.)

- Career exploration is a three-step process: (1) identify *your* personal skills, knowledge, abilities, interests and work-related values; (2) determine a career path or goal appropriate to *you*; and (3) follow proven procedures for obtaining *your* career goal.

HOW IS THIS BOOK ORGANIZED?

- *SECTION I: INTRODUCTION TO CAREER STRATEGIES* begins the discussion of criminal justice career opportunities by focusing on *you, the reader.* In **Chapter 1**, the reader has the opportunity to assess his/her own skills, knowledge, abilities, interests and values. Then, **Chapter 2** assists the reader in applying these assessment results to the setting of appropriate career goals.

- *SECTION II: LAW ENFORCEMENT CAREERS* is comprised of three chapters. **Chapter 3** defines the employment opportunities at the local, regional, county and Ohio-levels and how these opportunities parallel *your* career goals. Rather than let a career opportunity go undetected, a brief discussion of the employment outlook and federal law enforcement careers is also included. **Chapter 4** discusses private law enforcement opportunities. **Chapter 5** identifies and addresses preparation for the traditional law enforcement testing process.

- *SECTION III: CORRECTIONS CAREERS* is also comprised of three chapters. **Chapter 6** defines corrections-related employment opportunities at the local, regional, county and Ohio-levels. Again, a brief discussion of the employment outlook and federal law enforcement careers is also included. **Chapter 7** discusses privatization of corrections, while **Chapter 8** details the hiring procedures for the corrections field.

- *SECTION IV: EMPLOYMENT STRATEGIES* starts with **Chapter 9** and the necessity for an effective, planned, job-search strategy. Following an investigation-format of *what, who, where, when, how much,* and *how*, the reader can logically develop his or her *own* job-search strategy. **Chapter 10** identifies applicable employment laws, from federal civil rights acts and protections to Ohio Civil Service laws and lawful/unlawful employment topics. **Chapter 11** begins by comparing the needs and preferences of the employer to those of the prospective employee. Then, lays the foundation for the development of a resume by assisting the reader in identifying applicable and transferable skills. Resume format and procedures for drafting a resume follow, and the chapter ends with a discussion and sample of cover letters. **Chapter 12** assists the job-seeker in preparing for the job interview: from dress and types of interviews to appropriate communication styles and body language, sample questions, and suggested responses and post-interview follow-up.

- *SECTION V: WHAT HAPPENS AFTER…?* begins with **Chapter 13** addressing the critical question of, "What happens after…?" Now that *you* have been hired in the law enforcement field, what can you expect? What is the police subculture and how does it effect a new employee? The workbook concludes with **Chapter 14** discussing, "what happens after *you* have been hired in the corrections field? What can you expect? What is the inmate subculture and how can it effect *you*?

 **A Word of Caution:** by reading this book, you have taken a crucial step in the criminal justice employment process. This process is detailed and painstaking. The results rest with *you!* The more effort and careful consideration given to *your* career planning, the more effective *your* choice of *your* career will be.

ABOUT THE AUTHORS

Katherine A. Steinbeck is a Professor and Program Director for the Criminal Justice Program (Corrections and Law Enforcement) of Lakeland Community College in Kirtland, Ohio. She has over 10 years of practical experience in both private and public law enforcement and has held many positions, including police officer, police and private detective, crime prevention officer, C.A.L.E.A. accreditation coordinator and Director of Safety and Security for Bryn Mawr College in Pennsylvania. With over 15 years experience as a State of Ohio certified police academy instructor and 12 years, community college-level instructor, Ms. Steinbeck has presented workshops on the local-, state-, national- and international level. A certified crime prevention specialist in Ohio and Pennsylvania and publish author, she holds a Master's in Science, Technical Education degree from the University of Akron and a Bachelor's in Sociology/Criminology, from Miami University of Ohio. She is a member of the Academy of Criminal Justice Sciences, the American Association of University Women, Midwestern Criminal Justice Association and Ohio Women's Law Enforcement Network. She also founded the Ohio Women Criminal Justice Professors' Network and was only the second woman President of the Ohio Council of Criminal Justice Education in over 40 years of the council's existence.

Daniel F. Ponstingle has over 30 years experience as a past practitioner and both academic and training instructor in the law enforcement and corrections field. Recently retired as Director of the Criminal Justice Program at Lorain County Community College in Elyria, Ohio, he has also been an adjunct instructor with Lakeland Community College, Cuyahoga Community College and David N. Myers University. He combines his experience as a former commander and instructor of the Ohio Basic Peace Officer and Private Police Officer Academies with serving as liaison and ex-officio member of the Corrections Education Advisory Committee at Lorain County Community College, working in tandem with the Lorain and Grafton Correctional Institutions to provide corrections officer education. Mr. Ponstingle began his law enforcement career with the Detroit Police Department as a police officer and was promoted to research and development specialist before moving to Ohio. His active Ohio law enforcement experience includes tenure as Agent-in-Charge of the Lake County Narcotics Agency, being a licensed private investigator and certified American Bar Association Legal Assistant/Paralegal. He holds a Master's of Science degree from Central Michigan University and a Bachelor's of Science, from Wayne State University. He is a member of several professional organizations, including the Ohio Association of Chiefs of Police, Academy of Criminal Justice Sciences, Midwestern Criminal Justice Association and Ohio Council of Criminal Justice Education.

CHAPTER 1

DO YOU CHOOSE A CAREER OR

DOES IT CHOOSE YOU?

...Mighty things from small beginnings grow. -A. Mirabilis

AFTER READING THIS CHAPTER, YOU SHOULD KNOW
⇨ What are skav's.
⇨ Who you are.
⇨ What skills you have.
⇨ What workplace knowledge you possess.
⇨ What abilities and talents you have.
⇨ What personality type you are.
⇨ Whether you are left- or right-brained.
⇨ What you value most in your life.

INTRODUCTION

The Mid-West has a reputation for a strong work ethic. Ohioans spend considerable time and effort at work: we define ourselves by our careers and jobs. To include information or scales designed to elicit feedback about how important work is in your life would be superfluous and waste time. You know how important work is in your life without examining Maslow's Hierarchy of Human Needs. It's a given you're looking for a satisfying and appropriate workplace: you even bought a book to help you define your work-related needs and goals.

But, while you know the importance work plays in your life, have you examined *what* work you are capable of performing? Before you begin any career or job search, it is imperative you appreciate why you need to know your skav's. In criminal justice terms, your **skav's are skills, knowledge, abilities (including talents) and values**: the human resource equivalent of specifications for hiring, retaining, training and promoting criminal justice practitioners. If *you* don't know your skav's, how can you expect a prospective employer to know--and value--them? This chapter assists *you* in identifying your skav's. What are they? How do your skills, knowledge, abilities and values impact on your choice of career, employers and co-workers?

WHO ARE YOU?

? **What a question!** Why is this question in an employment workbook? In *Hamlet*, Shakespeare wrote, "…To thine own self be true…." The better you know yourself, the more closely matched your career goals and actual career. Take a moment and write down the answers to the following questions.

? If I were asked to describe myself, I'd say I was the kind of person who_____

_____

_____

_____

? I can spend hours and hours _____

_____

_____

? I believe my greatest accomplishment is_____

_____

_____

? My "dream" job is_____

_____

? I've started preparing for my new career by_____

_____

_____

WHAT ARE YOUR SKILLS?

☑ **Check the following skills which apply to you:**

☐ I demonstrate effective written communication skills.
☐ I am comfortable speaking in front of a group.
☐ I have effective interpersonal communication skills.
☐ I'm good at organizing projects--breaking down large project into measurable tasks.
☐ I'm good at organizing people--identify people and delegate tasks to appropriate people.
☐ I am effective administrative skills and can keep people on task.
☐ I excel at time-management skills and can complete tasks within deadlines.
☐ I have developed research skills--I can investigate projects and issues.
☐ I have administrative skills re scheduling, staffing etc....
☐ I have proven leadership skills and can delegate and accept responsibility.
☐ I am adept at mechanical-related projects.
☐ I have experience with animals esp. dog and/or horse.
☐ I can fix a motor vehicle or motorcycle.,
☐ I have experience with operating watercraft and/or bicycles.
☐ I have proven problem-solving skills.
☐ I am people-oriented.
☐ I have demonstrated resourcefulness and/or creativity on past projects.
☐ I believe in being a team-player.
☐ I am self-motivated and effective working alone.

WHAT WORKPLACE KNOWLEDGE DO YOU POSSESS?

Workplace knowledge is learned by four methods: formal education (high school co-operative program, associate's degree, bachelor's degree); through in-service training (police- or corrections-based academy); on-the-job training (during your probationary period) or via personal research and experience. Higher education is more than a preferred qualification for a prospective criminal justice employee: it promotes diversity of thought and relationships, reduces the likelihood of costly civil suits and is expected in a civil servant. From a more practical standpoint, many criminal justice employers give preferential hiring to associate- and baccalaureate-level graduates.

In-service and on-the-job training vary considerably from employer to employer. The Ohio Basic Police Academy will be discussed in Chapter 5 and corrections-based academies, in Chapter 8. Consequently, their remains the examination of knowledge you have learned through your own research and/or workplace experience.

☺ **Circle the following criminal justice-based knowledge areas in which you are proficient:**

☺ English (reports, public speaking, evidence, logs, etc....)
☺ Science (forensics, evidence, environmental, etc....)
☺ Math (reports, evidence, traffic reconstruction, inventory control, etc....)
☺ Sociology (how people interact)
☺ Psychology (why people act and interact)
☺ Victim-related Theories (trauma syndrome, responses to and treatments for, etc....)
☺ Criminal justice system itself (how the components interact)
☺ Criminal law (Ohio statutes, local ordinances)
☺ Criminal justice procedure (booking, testifying, evidentiary considerations, etc....)
☺ Policing (reality versus myth, community policing versus traditional, etc....)
☺ Private law enforcement (guard vs. officer, opportunities, etc....)
☺ Courts (3-levels, misdemeanor versus felony, etc....)
☺ Community-based corrections (probation, house arrest, reporting centers, etc....)
☺ Institutional corrections (jail versus prison, levels of security, etc....)
☺ Privatization of corrections (re community- and institutional-based)
☺ Juvenile justice and delinquency (status versus delinquency, one-pot jurisdiction, etc...)

WHAT ABILITIES & TALENTS DO YOU POSSESS?

How many of these criminal justice-based abilities and talents apply to you?

? Serious	? Conventional-thinker	? Adventurous
? Realistic	? Original-thinker	? Ambitious
? Detail-oriented	? Talkative	? Efficient
? Responsible	? Reserved	? Obedient
? Decisive	? Independent	? Practical
? Dedicated	? Curious	? Leader
? Conscientious	? Persistent	? Intuitive
? Analytical	? Critical	? Friendly

WHAT PERSONALITY TYPE ARE YOU?

Why does it matter which personality type you are? Consider the following situations. If you were the employee, would you feel comfortable in this workplace situation?

- ☹ You are reserved and prefer to work alone. Your employer requires every employee to have a partner...for all activities. To make matters worse, your new partner wants to be your buddy and know everything about you...immediately.

- ☹ You are friendly, talkative and sociable. Your employer assigns you to a position where you sit alone, all shift, and only interact with people long enough to check their identification.

- ☹ You believe in being thorough, practical, and working through your project step-by-step. Your employer wants you to get together with the other people on your shift to brainstorm ideas for the new mission statement.

- ☹ You prefer to be the "idea-person", offer theories and abstract thinking. Your employer assigns you to define a detailed plan--including enforcement of deadlines--for the new standard operating procedure manual.

- ☹ You prefer to work as a member of a team, with information flowing between ranks and shifts. Your employer maintains a strict span of control, requiring written authorization before you can approach the next ranking officer in the chain of command.

- ☹ You prefer to be on-the-move, active, observant, interacting with people. Your employer assigns you to standard duty, involving records management.

HOW DO YOU FIND YOUR PERSONALITY TYPE?

- ☞ Ask your friends and relatives. They're probably more than willing to give you a frank assessment of your personality--assets and liabilities.

- ☎ Call you past or current employer. If you have a positive, effective working relationship with that employer, you should receive honest, effective insight.

- ✓ Check copies of past performance evaluations for "good" and "bad" workplace-related qualities and interaction.

- ♭ Go to your local community college's counseling or career development center and ask for assistance in determining your personality type.

✋ Go to your local public library and review the Myers-Briggs Personality Sorter or Kiersey Temperament Sorter II (Myers-Briggs without the computer grading system).

📁 Visit Kiersey Temperament Sorter II at http://www.advisorteam.com/user/kcs.asp Enneagram (different sorter) at http://www.9types.com/

ARE YOU LEFT- OR RIGHT-BRAINED?

Take this quiz to determine if you are predominately left- or right-brained.

1. Do you like to do things one step at a time?
2. Do you frequently daydream?
3. Do you remember words and numbers better than you remember body language and colors?
4. Do you prefer logic and order over "warm fuzzies" and giving/receiving hugs?
5. Do you believe there is only "one right way" to do an activity?
6. Do you try to change life to meet your needs, even if it means not following the rules, step-by-step?
7. When taking a test, do you remember where the answer is in the book and what picture accompanied it?
8. When taking a test, do you remember the symbols and wording to the answer?
9. Has anyone said you were "blunt" because you prefer to follow the rules, be efficient and start the project, rather than just sit around and talk about completing the project?
10. Do you respond more to the message of a conversation, rather than the body language and tone of the speaker?

How did you do? The more "yes" answers you have, the more LEFT brained you are. If you have an equal number of "yes" and "no" answers, either: you're confused (re-think your answers) or you truly use both sides of your brain. If you're the latter, congratulations, you should be a great conversationalist!)

LEFT BRAIN   vs.   RIGHT BRAIN CHARACTERISTICS

1. Processes one step at a time
2. "Rooted" in reality, stable
3. One right way to do things
4. Responds to symbols, numbers, order, logic of the situation

1. Processes through visualization
2. Sings, jokes, daydreams
3. Change life to meet own needs
4. Responds to body language, tone, colors, aromas, emotions

Adapted from http://www.eiu.edu/~edtech/team Teach_Ex/index.htm (n.d.) and Gibbs. (n.d.). http://www.mtsu.edu/~devstud/advisor/brainta.html

DO YOU WANT A BETTER BALANCE BETWEEN LEFT-BRAIN & RIGHT-BRAIN?

Each half of the brain is controlled by the opposite side of the body. Therefore, to stimulate left brain activity, you need to activate the right side of your body. In other words, "only lefties are in their right mind!"

TO TURN ON YOUR LEFT- OR   RIGHT-BRAIN

1. Listen with your right ear	1. Listen with your left ear
2. Use your right hand more	2. Use your left hand more
3. Cross right leg/arm over left. (Turns right ear to speaker.)	3. Cross left leg/arm over right: (Turns left ear to speaker.)
4. Ask questions, take notes.	4. Doodle, do unstructured activity
5. Analyze/evaluate body language	5. Practice using positive self-talk
6. Demonstrated by list making	6. Demonstrated by empathy

WHAT DO YOU VALUE MOST IN YOUR LIFE?

Our lives are spent balancing the disparate roles we play. Are we ethical individuals? Are our needs and values more important than anyone else's? Can we balance the role of friend versus family member? Do we put the needs of family above our own? What happens when the role of family member conflicts with the role of employee? Does the family take precedent over our employer and organizational values? Do we have a responsibility to support and improve our community?

How you answer they questions give insight into your values and ethical philosophies. Take a moment to evaluate your own beliefs and values by writing down your responses to the following questions.

WHAT ARE YOUR VALUES?

My Values 1. Do I prefer to set my own standards?_____

_____

My Values 2. Do I believe in following my own standards?_____

_____

My Values 3. Do I often do things of which I'm ashamed?_____

_____

My Values 4. Do I admit my mistakes?_____

_____

My Values 5. How far am I willing to go to correct my mistakes?_____

_____

My Values 6. Do I often put the well-being of others ahead of my own?_____

_____

My Values 7. Am I honest?_____

_____

My Values 8. Do people respect my integrity?_____

_____

My Values 9. What is the most dishonest thing I've ever done?_____

_____

My Values 10. What is the most honest thing I've ever done?_____

_____

WHAT ARE YOUR FAMILY-RELATED VALUES?

The structure and dynamics of each family is unique. Family can be related by sanguinity (blood) or consanguinity (mutual definition and respect). There are single-parent households, nuclear families, extended families and partnerships. Consequently, as you complete the following questions, choose your answers on the basis of *your* definition of family. After all, the purpose of this workbook--and, especially this chapter--is to have *you* explore *your* skills, knowledge, abilities, and values. No one else's.

Family 1. How important is my family?_____

_____

Family 2. How many minutes per week do I spend talking with my children or parents?

_____

_____

Family 3. How many minutes per week do I spend talking with my spouse or partner?

_____

_____

Family 4. Does my family talk to me about their problems?_____

_____

Family 5. What activities do I regularly share with my family?_____

_____

Family 6. When was did the whole family do something together, just for the fun?_____

_____

Family 7. Can I name 5 of my spouse/partner's friends? _____

_____

Family 8. Can I name 5 of my children's friends?_____

_____

_____

Family 9. Are my family members getting enough kindness and sympathy from me? Can I give 2 examples of acts of kindness toward **each** family member?

_____

_____

_____

Family 10. When was the last time I told my family I loved them?_____

_____

CONCLUSION

Congratulations! By completing the contents of this chapters, you've performed a practical, in-depth analysis and evaluation of your skills, knowledge, abilities, talents and values. You've defined and examined your dreams and needs in the context of your learning style (left- or right-brained) and personality type. The next step in the planning of your career strategy is to review Chapter 2 and identify your occupational needs, choices and goals.

SUGGESTED READING

Enneagram (personality sorter). (n.d.). http://www.9types.com/

Kiersey Temperament Sorter II. (n.d.). http://www.advisorteam.com/user/kcs.asp

REFERENCES

Gibbs, Bill. (n.d.). *How Do We Learn? Learning theories: Right and left brain thinking survey.* Retrieved July 20, 2002, from Eastern Illinois University, Department of Media Services Web site: http://www.eiu.edu/~edtech/teamTeach_Ex/index.htm

Hemispheric Dominance Inventory. Retrieved July 20, 2002, from Middle Tennessee State University, The Developmental Studies Advising Center Web Site: http://www.mts.edu/~devstud/advisor/brainta.html

CHAPTER 2

CHASING CAREER CHOICES

...ought I to slacken the pace when approaching the goal?
Ought I not rather to put on speed?   -Diogenes

AFTER READING THIS CHAPTER, YOU SHOULD KNOW
⇨ How to identify potential career choices.
⇨ How to conduct a structured, career-related interview.
⇨ What you want from work.
⇨ What you want from your employer.
⇨ How to choose your employer.
⇨ How do you pick a "good" employer.
⇨ How to set your career goals.

INTRODUCTION

Having completed Chapter 1 and your in-depth self-evaluation, you are facing two divergent paths. You may believe you've hit a brick wall and don't know how to proceed. If this is case, take a moment to review how much you've learned. You now know your personality type, left- or right-brain dominated learning style and have gained considerable insight into your individual set of skills, knowledge, abilities and values. In other words, you now have an *internal* locus of control, grounded in your own character.

Conversely, having completed that same self-evaluation, you may feel the need to rush into a career, immediately take classes, tests, complete job applications. If so, remember the first criminal justice rule of a crisis--and, you *are* in crisis or you would not be reading this book--*"SLOW THINGS DOWN!"* If you *still* want to rush blindly ahead, then you obviously don't need to address such issues as how to choose an appropriate organizational culture, prospective employer, and group of co-workers? What *exactly* are you willing to give up for a job or career? Finally, how do you set your career goals?

IDENTIFYING POTENTIAL CAREER CHOICES

| LEFT-BRAINERS | VS. | RIGHT-BRAINERS |

LEFT-BRAINERS   VS.   **RIGHT-BRAINERS**

1. Study career guides

2. List choices from career guides

3. Read books on specific careers

4. Intern (structured learning, usually part-time and unpaid)

5. Work part-time re career choice

6. Become a member of a professional Association (check phone book, news-letters, The American Society of Crim-inology http://www.asc41.com

7. Take career exploration classes (public Libraries; on-line; career guidance centers; those sponsored by your city)

8. Study Occupational Outlook Handbook http://www.bls.gov/oco

9. Review http://www.hotjobs.com

10. Research United States government jobs http://www.usajobs.opm.gov/

11. Review potential company's annual

12. Conduct structure interview (next four pages)

---

1. Doodle your "ideal" career

2. Ask friends to suggest careers

3. Ask mentors to suggest careers

4. Job-Shadow (be someone's shadow at their workplace for a day)

5. Volunteer re career choice

6. Attend meetings of professionals (ask a teacher, check professional associations, Chamber of Commerce, college career center....)

7. Audit classes (technical centers; on-line; career and college guidance centers; public libraries)

8. Skim Occupational Outlook Handbook http://www.bls.gov/oco

9. Browse http://www.monster.com

10. View United States government jobs http://www.usajobs.opm.gov/

11. Directly contact local employer

12. Use structured interview form (next four pages)

CONDUCTING A STRUCTURED, CAREER-RELATED INTERVIEW

DIRECTIONS: Contact the criminal justice professional of your choice. Schedule an interview at the worksite, to better understand the workplace environment.

I.   JOB TITLE & REQUIREMENTS

A.   What is your job title?_____

B.   How many years of education are required for your job?_____

C.   Did your education help you get or keep your job? Why/why not?_____

_____

_____

D.   What training (academy, in-service, certification) is necessary for your job?

_____

E.   How long was this training/certification process?_____

_____

F.   Was the training/certification process completed as part of a probationary period? If so, how long was the probationary period?_____

_____

G.   Are there any physical requirements for the performance of your job? If so, should I be getting ready for these now? Why/why not?

_____

_____

CONDUCTING A STRUCTURED, CAREER-RELATED INTERVIEW (CONTINUED)

II. PERSONALITY, SOCIAL & FAMILY FACTORS

A. What personal characteristics and values would enable a person to do well at your job? Why? _____

_____

_____

B. What do your friends and family think about your line of work?_____

_____

_____

C. Is there any person in particular who influenced your job or career decision? If so, how did they influence your decision?_____

_____

_____

III. TASKS, DUTIES & WORKING CONDITIONS

A. How would you describe a "typical" day of work?_____

_____

_____

B. Would say your job is "more varied" or "more routine"? Why?_____

_____

C. What are your favorite parts of the job? Why?_____

_____

_____

CONDUCTING A STRUCTURED, CAREER-RELATED INTERVIEW (CONTINUED)

D. What are your least favorite parts of the job? Why?_____

_____

_____

E. What machines (cameras, VCR, breathalyzer...) and tools (handcuffs, weapons, pepper spray, walkie talkies...) do you use on your job? Should I be learning to use these now? Why/why not?_____

_____

_____

_____

F. What computer-related technology and software do you use? Should I be learning to use these now? Why/why not?_____

_____

_____

IV. FINANCIAL, BENEFITS & PROMOTIONAL STRUCTURE

A. How long have you been working on this job?_____

B. What is the current, entry-level salary or range for a person in your job?

_____

C. Who evaluates your work?_____

D. How often are you evaluated?_____

E. Does you evaluation effect your salary? Why/why not?_____

_____

F. How do you get a promotion? When/how often can you apply for one?___

_____

_____

G. Do you receive tuition reimbursement? If so, what is the reimbursement procedure? If not, would you be interested in this benefit? Why/why not?

_____

_____

_____

H. What other benefits does your job offer? (Example: life and medical insurance; vacation; sick leave; recreational membership; company car....)

_____

_____

_____

I. What benefit(s) would you like to receive that you're currently missing?

_____

V. JOB MARKET OVERVIEW

A. If there were a job opening today, would you have a lot of competition for that job opening? Why/why not?_____

_____

B. Do I have to relocate now to get hired at your job? Why/why not?_____

_____

CONDUCTING A STRUCTURED, CAREER-RELATED
INTERVIEW (CONTINUED)

C.   If I were hired for your job, would I have to relocate or transfer in the future? If so, how often?_____

D.   Should I be joining a particular association or club now? Why/why not?

_____

_____

E.   Does it hurt my chances in being hired if I don't have direct work experience in your field? Why/why not?_____

_____

_____

F.   Can I volunteer at your organization, department or agency? Why/why not?_____

_____

_____

G.   What aspects of my character or life could make it difficult for me to get hired at your organization, department or agency? Why?_____

_____

_____

H.   What final words of advice can you give me which would help me get hired in this field?_____

_____

_____

VI.   *"THANK YOU FOR GRANTING ME THIS INTERVIEW!"*

WHAT DO YOU WANT FROM YOUR EMPLOYER?

By now, you should have a better understanding of what you want from **work**: a job or a career. Perhaps, through the use of the structured interview, you have also formed an image of the kind of work you would (or wouldn't) like to do. But, do you know exactly what you want from an employer?

☑ **Check the following statements which you believe should apply to your prospective employer:**

☐ "I expect to receive financial pay and benefits as fits my experience."
☐ "I expect to receive competitive (standard rates) financial pay and benefits."
☐ "I prefer to keep my private life, private."
☐ "I prefer to integrate my private into the family created by the employer/job."
☐ "I'm willing to relocate my residency to the organization's city."
☐ "A good employer will take into consideration the employee's family-related needs."
☐ "A good employer will understand that family comes first, not the job."
☐ "A good employer will schedule me so I have enough time for my partner/spouse."
☐ "A good employer will schedule me so I have enough time for my children."
☐ "It's important for me to have a steady schedule, so I can accept social invitations."
☐ "My pets are important to me, so I don't want to be away from home too much."
☐ "My personal health should be a concern of my employer."
☐ "An effective executive communicates responsibly and informs employees of major changes."
☐ "I need to know I'll get credit for the work I do."
☐ "It's nice to receive a pat-on-the-back, every once in a while."
☐ "I prefer to be recognized for only the work where I've exceeded expectations."
☐ "A good employer should assist employee's in personal growth and renewal."
☐ "A good employer should financially assist an employee in lifelong learning."
☐ "An employer should demonstrate commitment to diversity by hiring minorities."
☐ "An employer should demonstrate commitment to diversity by retaining and promoting minorities."
☐ "A good employer helps the employee give back to the community."
☐ "A criminal justice-based employer should know that problems in the community result in problems for the department, organization or agency."
☐ "A job is just a job."
☐ "I don't want just a job, I want a career."

HOW DO YOU PICK A "GOOD" EMPLOYER?

Logically, a "good" employer should meet all or the majority of the employment-related statements you identified in the previous exercise. However, the previous statements are "wish-fulfillment", the ideal responses in an ideal employer. Reality may be more abrupt and certainly, less than ideal. So, we beg the question again: "How do you pick a good employer?" Relying on our academic roots, our recommendation is, of course: "Do you homework *before* you accept a position." Research the prospective employer's **organizational culture** or **the integrated pattern of...behavior that includes thoughts, speech, actions and artifacts (Shusta, 1995, pp.367-394).** When the results of the following research areas are examined, you will have determined the prospective organization's culture. If the results parallel the values you defined in Chapter 1, the prospective employer would be a "good" employer for you.

HOW DO YOU PICK AN ORGANIZATION'S THOUGHTS?

Evidence of a prospective organization's **thoughts** can be located in the organization's formal **speech**. In other words, research the organization's written documents and communication process to gain insight into organizational thoughts and values.

☑ **Check the organization's mission statement.** A mission statement is the organization's "reason for being" and can identify the organization's goals, values and relationship with the community. This evidence of the organization's thought process can be found in the organization's brochure, annual report, website, letterhead or standard operating procedures (manual).

    A.   What is the organization's mission statement?_____

_____

_____

    B.   Do is include values? If so, do the organization's values match the values you identified in Chapter 1? _____

_____

C. What is the general tone of the mission statement? Does it emphasize (list at or toward the beginning) traditional or community-oriented values? (Read the following comparison for assistance in identifying emphasis.)

TRADITIONAL	vs.	COMMUNITY-ORIENTED
1. Cynical, negative tone		1. Hopeful, positive tone
2. Emphasizes protection		2. Emphasizes services
3. Unwillingness to change		3. Willingness to change
4. Lead community		4. Partnership with community
5. Heavy on statistics, esp. re crime and response to crime		5. Heavy on values, esp. re supporting community

D. Therefore, the overall tone of the mission statement is?_____

E. Does this tone parallel your values as identified in Chapter 1? Why/why not?_____

F. Is there support for **social responsibility? Yes/no.** (Social responsibility is "…the recognition that organizations have significant influence on the social system" (Ohio Peace Officer Training Council, 1994, III-8, Overhead #6)

☑ **Check the table of organization.** The table of organization is a chart or which diagrams the ranks and divisions of the organization. There are two primary styles of organization:

A.
TRADITIONAL STYLE	vs.	COMMUNITY-ORIENTED
1. Tall hierarchy: many layers & divisions in chain of command command		1. Flat hierarchy: few layers divisions in chain of
2. EX: officer, corporal, sergeant, lieutenant, captain, chief executive		2. EX: officer, sergeant, chief executive
3. Majority are specialists		3. Majority are generalists
4. So, promotional opportunities are available		4. So, majority are cross-trained jobs, but few promotions
5. Communication slow on way up		5. Communication fast on way up
6. Only communicate within divisions or through commanders		6. Communicate within established system

B. Therefore, the table of organization is which style?_____

C.   Does the table of organization styles match what you want from work? Why/why not?_____

_____

ACTIONS SPEAK LOUDER THAN WORDS!

Do the **actions** of the organizational culture support or contradict the stated mission, table of organization? What is the overall public image of the organization and why is this important? *Why* would you knowingly seek employment with an organization with a less-than-stellar public image? If the organization has a reputation for not following through on projects and/or not demonstrating integrity and loyalty to the community it serves, why should the organization treat you well? Couldn't the organization's poor image be a problem for your job security? For your professional recognition and self-actualization?

To determine the answers to the following questions, interview area residents; research printed organizational reports and brochures; read the local newspaper (print or electronic); watch the local news channel and, if possible, ask organizational employees. The research is not difficult, though it may be time-consuming. But, as a popular advertisement states, "Aren't you worth it?"

Consider your prospective employer. How would you answer the following questions about that organization's actions and behaviors?

💣 Does the mission statement sound community-oriented, but the actions of the organization are traditional?

💣 Does the community and organization's mission statement support diversity, but few minority employees have been hired?

💣 If the community and organization have hired minority employees, have minority employees been *promoted?*

💣 Does the organization match people and jobs? (For instance, does the job posting list the skav's (skills, knowledge, abilities, values) or only the preferred requirements?)

💣 If the organization seems traditional, do they still try to promote a community-organization partnership?

💣 How well does the organization deal with change, such as economic or demographic?

💣 Is there a citizen oversight committee? (For instance, is their a civilian review board, community association or volunteer organization which works with the organization?) If so, what is *their* opinion of the organization?

💣 Does the organization communicate responsibly (inform people of major decisions)?

💣 Does the chief executive "model the way" (exemplify best organizational values)?

💣 Is the organization professional? Has it earned any awards or accreditations?

💣 Are the actions of the organization ethical? Have there been any recent scandals?

WHAT'S AN ORGANIZATIONAL ARTIFACT?

An **artifact** is any tangible object that could be passed down to another generation. Therefore, an organizational artifact is an object belonging to the organization which can be used by and passed to subsequent employees. While this category is the smallest element of the organizational culture, you should still investigate whether or not the artifact's image matches that of the organization. For further insight, consider the following questions and remember that they apply to law enforcement *and* corrections organizations.

✓ Does the organization claim to be progressive, but is using outdated equipment?

✓ Does the organization claim to be professional, but, because of sloppy documentation and/or evidence processing, frequently lose in criminal or appellate court?

✓ Have you heard about a recent scandal or use of excessive force?

✓ Does the organization claim to serve the community, but the logo strongly supports traditional police enforcement or a correctional "lock-'em up" style of management?

✓ What photographs, charts, paintings or other images are on the walls of the organization's building?

✓ Are these posted images positive or negative images?

✓ Do these posted images support your value system?

✓ Bottom line: when you hear this organization's name, what images come to mind?

HOW DO YOU SET YOUR CAREER GOALS?

Use the information learned in this chapter to complete this chart:

WORKPLACE ISSUE	YOUR CONCLUSION
1. Potential career choices?	
2. Results of left/right-brain research?	
3. Preferred job title & requirements?	
4. Match with personality, social & family factors?	
5. Preferred tasks, duties, working conditions?	
6. Necessary financial, benefits & promotional structure?	
7. Current job market?	
8. What do you want from work? (Regarding family/friends? Regarding your needs?)	
9. How do you define a "good" employer?	
10. Results from "organizational thoughts" & "speech" research?	
11. Results from "organizational actions" research?	
12. Results from "organizational artifact" research?	

CONCLUSION

This chapter was particularly difficult in that you completed a realistic and illuminating critique of your dreams. To conclude this critique, however, three questions.

➤ First, after reviewing your dreams in the stark light of reality, are they still viable?

➤ Second, have you a better understanding of your career priorities and loyalties? For instance, have you decided who takes priority in a battle over conflicting duties and limited time, family or the organization? Does your list of priorities change when the conflict is between *friends* and the organization? Why/why not?

➤ Third, now what do you do? If the reality of your search matches your dreams, you've achieved success. You're on the right path and can proceed to the law enforcement chapters (chapters 3-5) or corrections (chapters 6-8). On the other hand, if your dream is in jeopardy, now what? First things first: *what* is the problem? Is the problem insurmountable or can it be remedied or removed? Will your dream simply take longer to follow? Can you afford the financial cost and stress-related effort this time delay will cause? If your family is against your pursuing your dream, are you willing to let them dictate your life or be a source of stress as you pursue your dream? Bottom line, *how much* do you want to pursue your dream? Before you decide to relinquish your dream, consider this poem:

> "I think continually of those who were truly great--
> The names of those who in their lives fought for life,
> Who wore at their hearts the fire's centre."
> -Stephen Spender's *I Think Continually of Those*

SUGGESTED READING

The American Society of Criminology. (n.d.). http://www.asc41.com

Job listings. (n.d.). http://hotjobs.com and http://monster.com

United States government job listings. (n.d.). http://usajobs.opm.gov/

REFERENCES

Ohio Peace Officer Training Council. (1994). *Ohio Peace Officer Basic Training Curriculum, Human Relations III-8, Cultural Sensitivity.* Columbus, Ohio: Ohio Attorney General's Office.

Shusta, R.M., Levine, D.R., Harris, P.R. & Wong, H.Z. (1995). *Multicultural law enforcement: Strategies for peacekeeping in a diverse society.* Englewood Cliffs, NJ: Prentice Hall.

CHAPTER 3

LOOKING AT PUBLIC LAW ENFORCEMENT

I think continually of those who were truly great--
The names of those who in their lives fought for life,
Who wore at their heart's their fire's centre.
-Stephen Spender

AFTER READING THIS CHAPTER, YOU SHOULD KNOW
⇨ What the employment numbers are for law enforcement.
⇨ Ohio law enforcement statistics.
⇨ Whether you want to make Ohio municipal law enforcement your home.
⇨ If you should consider county law enforcement.
⇨ What state-level agencies are in Ohio.
⇨ How federal law enforcement agencies are organized.

INTRODUCTION

In Chapter 1, you completed an in-depth analysis of your skills, knowledge, abilities, and values. In Chapter 2, you explored and defined your *general* career needs, choices, employer and organizational culture. Here, however, we'll review the *specifics* on law enforcement careers.

Many career guide books start by stating the obvious. Of course, law enforcement is a dangerous and stressful career. Obviously, it is not a standard 9 to 5 kind of occupation. Yes, one attraction is the job security. Realistically (and pessimistically), as long as there are people and laws, someone, somewhere will break the law; thereby, reinforcing the need for law enforcement procedures and officers. Naturally, there are many opportunities for advancement; but, contrary to urban legends, if you are seeking a position in public law enforcement, you usually start at an entry-level position.

But, what *specifically* is the occupational outlook for public law enforcement? What *specific* jobs are available at the local-, regional-, county-, state- and federal-levels? Lastly, what job is right for *you?*

WHAT ARE THE EMPLOYMENT NUMBERS?

In other words, will you be able to find employment in public law enforcement?

Consider the following *general* statistics from the *Occupational Outlook Handbook, 2002-2003, (12-31-01, News releases)*:

★ **Minority employment will rise**: Asians, 44 percent; Hispanics, 36 percent; Blacks, 21 percent and Whites, 9 percent (2000-2010 Employment projections).

★ **"...(T)he women's labor force will grow more rapidly than the men's** (2000-2010 Employment projections).

★ **Service-producing occupations** (firefighters, law enforcement and other protective services i.e. private law enforcement) **will remain the dominant employment,** generating 20.5 million jobs by 2010 (2000-2010 Employment projections).

★ **Service occupations will rise:** 19.5 percent between the years 2000 and 2010 (table 2) or 1.8 percent each year (table 1).

★ **Retirements are pending.** By 2010, baby boomers (46-64 years old) are expected to be the "substantial share" of the labor force (2000-2010 Employment projections). But, that also means they will be retiring, opening new entry-level and promotional opportunities!

Specifically, according to the *Occupational Outlook Handbook, 2002-2003, Police and detectives*:

★ "Employment of police and detectives is expected in <u>increase faster than the average</u> for all occupations through 2010...(though) growth at the Federal level will be tempered by continuing budgetary constraints" (Job Outlook section, paragraph 2).

★ "Police and detectives held about 834,000 jobs in 2000. About 80 percent were employed by local governments. State police agencies employed about 13 percent and various Federal agencies employed about 6 percent" (Employment section, paragraph 1).

PUBLIC LAW ENFORCEMENT AGENCIES IN OHIO

A public law enforcement agency is considered a not-for-profit organization and one funded through public dollars, such as property taxes, tax levies and bonds. (Continue reading this chapter if you believe you want to work for public law enforcement.) Private law enforcement, on the other hand, is profit-oriented; but, in the business of law enforcement. (Read Chapter 4 for additional insights into private law enforcement opportunities.)

The second issue is whether you are interested in working for an **Ohio** public law enforcement agency. Just because you purchased a book on Ohio criminal justice careers, you are not required to limit your search to Ohio. So, let's keep an open mind and start by determining whether you want to work for public law enforcement in Ohio.

 OHIO LAW ENFORCEMENT STATISTICS

First, let's determine which of the following statements apply to *you*:

1. I'd rather belong to the largest group of law enforcement agencies.
2. I'd rather belong to the smallest group of law enforcement agencies.
3. An agency of over 25 or more employees is more appropriate for me.
4. I'd rather work for an agency of 25 or less employees.
5. I believe there should be a community-police partnership.
6. I believe it is more important to make arrests than keep the peace.
7. I want to be a generalist, a team-player, trained to do a variety of jobs in the agency.
8. I want to be a specialist, trained to do one job well, with plenty of opportunities for personal advancement and promotion.
9. An agency should investigate citizen allegations of misconduct themselves.
10. An agency should support an outside system of investigating allegations of misconduct.
11. I am a female candidate.
12. I am a person of color.

How did you do? Answers to Ohio Law Enforcement:

1 & 2: According to Williams, M. R., King, W. R., & Holcomb, J. E. (2001, p. 10): "As of 1996, the Bureau of Justice Statistics reported 938...agencies...composed of 808 municipal police departments (86.1 percent), 88 county sheriff offices (9.4 percent...), 41 special police agencies (4.4 percent...), and one State highway patrol."

3 & 4: Per Williams, M. R., King, W. R., & Holcomb, J. E. (2001, p. 10), "...in 1996, over 66 percent of public police departments in Ohio employed 25 or fewer employees."

5 & 6: Question #5 refers to a community-policing department and question #6, is a traditional department. "Of the 131 Ohio police agencies responding to a survey conducted by the Bureau of Justice Statistics in 1997, 72 percent reported having either a formal or informal Community Oriented Policing (COP) plan for their department" (Williams, M. R., King, W. R., & Holcomb, J. E., 2001, p. 10). For information on community policing, visit the National Center for Community Policing at Michigan State University: http://www.cj.msu.edu/~people/cp/

7 & 8: Again, Question #7 refers to community-policing and question #8, traditional-style of policing.

9 & 10: A department which investigates citizen allegations of police misconduct itself usually has an internal affairs department. An outside system for the investigation of citizen allegations usually means the department utilizes a civilian review board or CRB: a board staffed by citizens who hear complaints and issue findings on the complaints, such as the finding of no-fault, disciplinary action required, recommendation for termination of an employee and/or criminal prosecution. In 1997, "...3.8 percent reported having a CRB" (William, M. R., King, W. R., & Holcomb, J. E., 2001, p. 11).

11. "Of the 3, 355 U.S. law enforcement agencies surveyed by the Bureau of Justice Statistics in 1997, women comprised a mean of 7.7 percent of full-time sworn officers...(as compared to) 7.3 percent of full-time sworn officers in the 129 Ohio agencies responding to this same survey..." (William, M. R., King, W. R., & Holcomb, J. E., 2001, p. 11).

12. "Thirteen percent of full-time sworn officers in 3,355 U.S. law enforcement agencies (in 1997) were people of color. However, in Ohio during 1997, only 7 percent of sworn officers were people of color (William, M. R., King, W. R., & Holcomb, J. E., 2001, p. 11).

MAKING MUNICIPAL LAW ENFORCEMENT YOUR HOME

Typically, when you tell someone you're thinking of law enforcement as a career, the usual job which comes to mind is that of police officer. As previously discussed, the vast majority of the employment opportunities are in municipalities: over 800 in Ohio, alone!

But, did you consider the following aspects of a career in municipal policing?

☑ **Job openings:** "The number of qualified candidates…is inadequate to meet growth and replacement needs in many local and special police departments" (*Occupational Outlook Handbook, 2002-2003,* n.d. Police and detectives).

☑ **Helping profession:** "…80 percent of requests for police assistance do not involve crimes…" (Cole, G. F. & Smith, C. E., 1999, p. 87).

☑ **High School education:** "In 1997, 14% of local police departments…had some type of college education requirement for new officers" (*Bureau of Justice Statistics*, n.d., Education and training requirements). In other words, the majority of municipal police departments only require a high school education. Consequently, anyone with "some college" or at least a 2-year, associate's degree will have the competitive edge in both the written examination and oral interview steps of the hiring process.

☑ **Education bonus points on written exam:** "Additional credits to a maximum of 20% will be applied to the written test scores for those applicants with a passing score…(including) college degree two year (3%) or four year (6%)…." [City of Rocky River examination for entry level police officer, (2002, August 18), *The Plain Dealer,* Classifieds].

☑ **Residency bonus points on written exam:** If a municipal agency values local residency in its officer-candidates, the agency usually awards "bonus" points on the written examination results. For example, the City of Bedford Heights (Ohio) entry-level police officer examination advertisement [(2002, July 28), *The Plain Dealer*, Classifieds) grants extra points for one year residency.

☑ **Internet links for research:** Simply type in the name of the agency for which you want to work and visit their website. Additionally, the Ohio Association of Chiefs of Police, Inc website lists 36 law enforcement agencies and 18 other state, federal and law-related links at http://www.oacp.org or the Ohio Attorney General's Law Enforcement Links at http://www.ag.state.oh.us/links/lenlinks.htm

STOP & CONSIDER COUNTY LAW ENFORCEMENT!

County law enforcement is actually a combination of two vastly different categories of law enforcement agencies: regional and county. In Ohio, a regional law enforcement agency is a police agency with multiple jurisdictions (geographic responsibility) and enforcement responsibilities unique to their agency. Consequently, any search for a regional agency must be conducted on a region-by-region basis, rather than for the state of Ohio. **For example, here are three different northern Ohio regional law enforcement agencies:**

	CLEVELAND METROPARKS RANGER DEPARTMENT	**CUYAHOGA METROPOLITAN HOUSING AUTHORITY**	**REGIONAL TRANSIT AUTHORITY**
JURISDICTION	★ Park area ★ 5 Counties ★ 42 Munici-palities ★ 100+ miles of parkway	★ Housing ★ Cuyahoga County only ★ 35+ Estates	★ Transportation (bus, trains), tracks, shelters & stations ★ Greater Cleveland
EDUCATIONAL REQUIREMENT	High school	High school	High school
INTERNET ADDRESS	http://www.clemet parks.com/rangers. html	http://www.cmha.net/ cmhapolicedept/ cmhapolicedept.html	http://gcrta.org/ publicsafety.asp

County law enforcement, on the other hand, is comprised of three sub-categories: sheriff's departments, community colleges, and public hospitals. Ohio has **88 sheriff's departments** from which to choose a prospective employer. **Community colleges** appear to be county-based. However, they are primarily under Ohio-based procedures; funding; union regulations (State Employee Relations Board); retirement system (Public Employees Retirement System of Ohio); and Board of Regents accreditation system. Therefore, community colleges will be discussed under state law enforcement agencies.

Conversely, **public hospitals** remain under county jurisdiction. Be careful in researching the agency as a prospective employer. Because of politics, history, funding or image, public hospital law enforcement may still be listed under such anachronistic departmental names as "Security" or "Public Safety". Consequently, either telephone the switchboard and ask for the name and director of the agency or research the agency through the internet. (Review the chart on the next page for additional insight.)

32.

Examples of other county-based, law enforcement agencies in Ohio:

	PUBLIC HOSPITALS	**SHERIFF'S**
JURISDICTION	★ Business ★ Public hospital people, grounds, equipment, proprietary date (info)	★ Elected sheriff, hired deputy sheriffs ★ Rural area ★ Areas not already under jurisdiction of another law enforcement agency
EDUCATIONAL REQUIREMENT	High school, trend toward associate's degree	High school, trend toward associate's degree
RESEARCHING ON THE INTERNET ADDRESS	☹ Because of politics, resources, image, may still use "Security" ☺ Use site map to search for departmental name	☹ The sheriff is an elected official; so, be careful to use the name of the current sheriff. ☺ Ohio has 88 counties; so, 88 sheriffs or 88 prospective employers!
EXAMPLES	Cleveland Clinic at http://www.clevelandclinic.org or University Hospitals at http://www.uhhs.com	Specific county or via Buckeye State Sheriffs' Association at http://www.buckeysheriffs.org/

 STATE-LEVEL LAW ENFORCEMENT AGENCIES IN OHIO

There are two different organizational models for state-level law enforcement agencies. First, there are "state police" who enforce all state-level laws, without jurisdictional restrictions i.e. Texas Rangers. Ohio, conversely, is indicative of the second organizational model which weaves a network of highway patrol, parks, campus police and support organizations. (Read on for a comparison chart of state agencies.)

In other words, opportunities abound. According to the Bureau of Justice Statistics, from 1996-1999, the Ohio State Highway Patrol hired 7 percent more employees, 6 percent rise in sworn personnel and 9 percent, civilian (LEMAS, November, 2000, Table 1b).

Primary State of Ohio *law enforcement* agencies include:

	OHIO STATE HIGHWAY PATROL	OHIO DEPT. OF NATURAL RESOURCES	CAMPUS POLICE
JURISDICTION	★ State highways ★ State property (client or inmate abuse) ★ Protection of Secretary of State ★ Airplane crashes	★ State parks ★ Game & wildlife laws ★ Crimes against persons ★ Crimes against property	★ Community colleges ★ Public state colleges and universities ★ Balance law enforcement & college-re service
EDUCATIONAL REQUIREMENT	High school, associate's preferred	Recommend competitive edge of associate's degree (criminal justice). Bachelor's in criminal justice or parks & recreation, preferred.	Associate's degree for community colleges; bachelor's (criminal justice or public adminis-tration) for 4-year colleges and universities.
INTERNET ADDRESSES	http://www.state.oh.us/ohiostate patrol OR toll free, 1-888-TROOPER	http://www.dnr.state.oh.us/wildlife/employ/default.htm	Ohio Campus Law Enforcement Association @ http://www3.uakron.edu/police/oclea/oclea.htm

Primary State of Ohio *law enforcement support* agencies include:

	BUREAU OF CRIMIN-AL IDENTIFICATION & INVESTIGATION	GOVERNOR'S OFFICE OF CRIMINAL JUSTICE SERVICES
JURISDICTION	★ State Crime Lab ★ Special Investigations, like Computer Crime Unit	★ Special investigators ★ Crime prevention ★ Information & education
EDUCATIONAL REQUIREMENT	Bachelor's degree in field of expertise (criminal justice or science)	Bachelor's degree in field of expertise (criminal justice or education)
INTERNET ADDRESS	http://www.ag.state.oh.us/bci/bcii.htm	http://www.ocjs.state.oh.us/

A WORD ABOUT FEDERAL LAW ENFORCEMENT AGENCIES

A discussion of law enforcement careers would not be complete without the inclusion of federal-level opportunities. Competition for federal employment is fierce and employment-related issues, unique.

 **FEDERAL LAW ENFORCEMENT FACTS**

☹ **Limited job openings:** "The number of qualified candidates exceed the number of job openings in Federal and State law enforcement agencies" (*Occupational Outlook Handbook 2002-2003*, n.d., Police and detectives, Significant points).

💣 **Re-organizations:** Fall-out from the domestic terrorism incidents of September 11, 2001, should result in re-organizations of federal agencies; but, it is too premature to speculate what impact those re-organizations will have on employment opportunities.

💣 **Budgetary restraints:** "…employment growth at the Federal level will be tempered by continuing budgetary constraints faced by law enforcement agencies" (*Occupational Outlook Handbook 2002-2003,* n.d., Police and detectives, Job Outlook).

☑ **Baccalaureate (bachelor's) degree required:** "Federal…agencies typically require a college degree" (*Occupational Outlook Handbook 2002-2003,* n.d., Police and detective, Training, and Other Qualifications, and Advancement). The more financial the crimes, the more an accounting or law degree is recommended.

☎ **Contact the pertinent agency regarding their foreign language preference:** Since bachelor's degree requirements usually include a foreign language, do your homework. Maximize your employability and competitive edge by carefully choosing the appropriate language for the pertinent agency.

✂ **Be prepared to cut ties to a particular location:** "The jobs of some Federal agents such as U.S. Secret Service and DEA special agents require extensive travel, often on very short notice. They may relocate a number of times over the course of their careers" (*Occupational Outlook Handbook 2002-2003,* n.d., Police and detective, Working Conditions).

◎ **Target the age requirements:** "In the Federal Government, candidates must be at least 21 years of age but less than 37 years of age at the time of appointment" (*Occupational Outlook Handbook 2002-2003,* n.d., Police and detectives, Training, Other Qualifications, and Advancement).

☺ **Consider the earning potential:** "Median (most frequently occurring) annual earnings of $44,000 in State government, $39,700 in local government, and $37,760 in Federal Government" (*Occupational Outlook Handbook 2002-2003,* n.d., Police and detectives, Earnings).

 FEDERAL LAW ENFORCEMENT OPPORTUNITIES

Federal Law Enforcement - Treasury Department:

	JURISDICTION	INTERNET ADDRESS
ATF/BUREAU OF ALCOHOL, TOBACCO & FIREARMS • **ATF Agent**	★ Enforce Federal firearms and explosive-re laws ★ Tax-re regulations	http://www.atf.treas.gov
IRS/INTERNAL REVENUE SERVICE	★ Enforce tax laws	http://www.treas.gov/jobs
U.S. CUSTOMS SERVICE • **Customs Agent**	★ Suppress narcotics smuggling ★ Money laundering ★ Child pornography ★ Customs fraud	http://www.customs.treas.gov/career/career.htm
• **Customs Inspector**	★ Inspect and enforce re imports/exports laws (people & vehicles)	Same as Customs Agent
U.S. SECRET SERVICE • **U.S. Secret Service Agent**	★ Investigate counter-feiting ★ Fraudulent use of credit cards ★ Protect President, VP, Presidential candidates, Past Presidents, visiting foreign dignitaries & all their immediate families	http://www.treas.gov/usss

(*Occupational Outlook Handbook 2002-2003,* n.d., Police and detectives).

Federal Law Enforcement - Department of Justice:

	JURISDICTION	INTERNET ADDRESS
DEA/DRUG ENFORCEMENT ADMINISTRATION	★ Enforcement re illegal drugs ★ Overseas drug-re investigations	http://www.usdoj.gov/dea
FBI/FEDERAL BUREAU OF INVESTIGATION	★ Organized crime ★ Public corruption ★ Financial crime ★ Bank robbery ★ Extortion ★ Kidnapping ★ Air piracy ★ Terrorism ★ Espionage ★ Interstate crimes	http://www.fbi.gov
INS/IMMIGRATION & NATURALIZATION SERVICE • **Border Patrol** -------------------- • **Immigration Inspectors**	★ 8,000 miles of international land and water boundaries ★ Smuggling ★ Unlawful entry -------------------- ★ Examine people seeking entrance to U.S. and territories	http://www.ins.usdoj.gov/ graphics/workfor/careers/ bpcareer/index.htm -------------------- Same as Border Patrol
U.S. MARSHALS SERVICE	★ Protect courts ★ Protect Federal judiciary ★ Transport Federal prisoners ★ Witness Protection ★ Pursue Federal fugitives	http://www.usdoj.gov/ marshals

(Occupational Outlook Handbook 2002-2003, n.d., Police and detectives).

Miscellaneous Federal Law Enforcement Agencies:

	JURISDICTION	INTERNET ADDRESS
U.S. POSTAL SERVICE • **Postal Inspectors**	★ Crimes conducted via U.S. mail	http://www.usps.com/ websites/depart/inspect/ welcome.htm
DEPT. OF TRANSPOR-ATION: • **U.S. Coast Guard**	★ Suppress contraband trade in U.S. waters ★ Rescue those in distress	http://www.uscg.mil/jobs/
FEDERAL AVIATION ADMINISTRATION • **Federal Air Marshals**	★ Suppress and investigate crimes re air transportation	http://jobs.faa.gov/
GENERAL SERVICES ADMINISTRATION • **Federal Protective Service**	★ Provide safety and security to Federal workers, buildings and property	http://www.usajobs.opm.gov/
U.S. DEPT. OF STATE, BUREAU OF DIPLOMATIC SECURITY	★ Terrorism ★ Overseas security ★ Protect Secretary of State	http://www.ds.state.gov/career
U.S. DEPT. OF THE INTERIOR • **Bureau of Indian Affairs**	★ Suppress and investigate crimes re BIA land, equipment, date and personnel	http://bialaw.fedworld.gov/
• **National Park Service**	★ Crimes re national park land, use, property, and personnel	http://www.nps.gov/ personnel

(*Occupational Outlook Handbook 2002-2003*, n.d. Police and detectives)

CONCLUSION

Fine-tuning an issue as important as your career aspiration is extremely difficult. First, you compared municipal, regional, county and state law enforcement agencies by examining their unique jurisdictional, educational requirements, and internet addresses.

Then, we further complicated your career focus by providing a comprehensive comparison of federal law enforcement agencies. If you are feeling overwhelmed and confused, do not despair. The rule in any crisis intervention situation is to slow things down. Do not make such an important decision as a career focus on a whim: do your homework, visit the websites we suggest under the following section, "Suggested Reading". Then, make an informed decision and choose a level of law enforcement which best meets your personal needs and professional goals.

SUGGESTED READING

Buckeye State Sheriffs' Association at http://www.buckeyesheriffs.org/

Bureau of Alcohol, Tobacco & Firearms at http://www.atf.treas.gov

Cleveland Clinic at http://clevelandclinic.org/

Cleveland Metroparks Ranger Department at http://clemetparks.com/rangers.html

Cuyahoga Metropolitan Housing Authority Police Department at http://www.cmha.net/cmhapolicedept/cmhapolicedept.html

Dept. of the Interior's Bureau of Indian Affairs at http://bialaw.fedworld.gov/

Dept. of the Interior's National Park Service at http://www.nps.gov/personnel

Dept. of Transportation, U.S. Coast Guard at http://www.uscg.mil/jobs/

Drug Enforcement Administration (DEA) at http://www.usdoj.gov/dea

Federal Aviation Administration's Civil Aviation Security Specialist (Federal Air Marshals) at http://jobs.faa.gov/

Federal Bureau of Investigation (FBI) at http://www.fbi.gov

General Services Administration's Federal Protective Service at http://www.usajobs.opm.gov/

Governor's Office of Criminal Justice Services at http://www.ocjs.state.oh.us/

Greater Cleveland Regional Transit Authority Public Safety Department at http://www.gcrta.org/publicsafety.asp

Immigration & Naturalization Service (INS) at http://www.ins.usdoj.gov/graphics/ workfor/careers/bpcareer/index.htm

International Association of Women Police at http://www.iawp.org

Internal Revenue Service (IRS) at http://www.treas.gov/jobs

National Center for Community Policing, Michigan State University at http://www.msu. edu/ ~people/cp/

Ohio Association of Chiefs of Police, Inc at http://www.oacp.org

Ohio Attorney General's Law Enforcement links at http://ag.state.oh.us/links/lenlinks.htm

Ohio Bureau of Criminal Identification & Investigation at http://www.ag.state.oh.us/bci/ bcii.htm

Ohio Campus Law Enforcement Association at http://www3.uakron.edu/police/oclea/ oclea.htm

Ohio Department of Natural Resources at http://www.dnr.state.oh.us/wildlife/employ/ default.htm

Ohio State Highway Patrol at http://www.state.oh.us/ohiostatepatrol/

Ohio Women's Law Enforcement Network at http://KBTrooper@ADL.com

University Hospitals at http://uhhs.com

U.S. Customs Service at http://www.customs.treas.gov/career/career.htm

U.S. Dept. of State, Bureau Diplomatic Security at http://www.ds.state.gov/career

U.S. Marshals Services at http://www.usdoj.gov/marshals

U.S. Postal Service at http://www.usps.com/websites/depart/inspect/welcome.htm

U.S. Secret Service at http://www.treas.gov/usss

Women in Federal Law Enforcement at http://www.ceeme.com/WIFLE/

REFERENCES

Bureau of Justice Statistics. (2000, November). *LEMAS/Law Enforcement Management and Administrative Statistics:* Individual State & Local Agencies with 100, Table 1b. Retrieved August 5, 2002, from http://

City of Bedford Heights entry level police officer examination. (2002, July 28). *The (Cleveland) Plain Dealer,* Classifieds.

City of Rocky River examination for entry level police officer. (2002, August 18). *The Plain Dealer,* Classifieds.

Cole, G. F. & Smith, C. E. (1999). *Criminal Justice.* Belmont, CA: Wadsworth Publishing Company.

LEMAS/Law Enforcement Management and Administrative Statistics. (2000, November). *Bureau of Justice Statistics: Individual state and local agencies with 100 or more officers.* Retrieved August 5, 2002, from http://www.ojp.usdoj.gov/bjs/abstract/lemas99.htm, Table 1b

Occupational Outlook Handbook, 2002-2003. (n.d.). *Police and detectives.* Retrieved September 1, 2002, from http://www.bls.gov/oco/ocos160.htm

Occupational Outlook Handbook, 2002-2003. (12-31-01). *News release, 2000-2010 Employment projections.* Retrieved September 1, 2002, from http://www.bls.gov/emp

Occupational Outlook Handbook, 2002-2003. (12-3-01). *News release, table 1. Employment by major industry division, 1990, 2000, and projected 2010.* Retrieved September 1, 2002, from http://www.bls.gov/news.release/ecopro.t02.htm

Occupational Outlook Handbook, 2002-2003. (12-31-01). *News release, table 2. Employment by major occupational group, 2000 and projected 2010.* Retrieved September 1, 2002, from http://www.bls.gov/news.release/ecopro.t02.htm

Williams, M. R., King, W. R., & Holcomb, J. E. (2001). *Criminal justice in ohio.* Needham Heights, MA: Allyn & Bacon.

CHAPTER 4

PRIVATE LAW ENFORCEMENT POSITIONS

Our similarities are different. -Yogi Berra

AFTER READING THIS CHAPTER, YOU SHOULD KNOW
⇨ What private law enforcement opportunities exist.
⇨ How private and public law enforcement compare.
⇨ The employment numbers for private law enforcement.
⇨ What earnings are possible in private law enforcement.
⇨ How to become a private investigator in Ohio.

INTRODUCTION

To be succinct, here are the answers to the most frequently asked questions:

1) **No, security officer is only one kind of job in the private law enforcement field: there are many other jobs in this field.** "Private security is a profit-oriented industry that provides personnel, equipment and/or procedures to *prevent* losses caused by human error, emergencies, disasters or criminal actions" (Hess, K. M., & Wrobleski, H. M., 1996, p. 29). Besides, the *Occupational Outlook Handbook*, 2002-2003 (n.d.) uses the occupational titles of "Security guards and gaming surveillance officers"; "Private detectives and investigators"; "Bill and account collectors"; "Claims adjusters"; "Appraisers" and "Examiners".

2) **No, you don't have to work for one company.** "**Proprietary services** are in-house, directly hired and controlled by the company or organization. In contrast, **contract services** are outside firms or individuals who provide security services for a fee. **Hybrid services** combine the two" (Hess, K. M., & Wrobleski, H. M., 1996, p. 37).

3) **Yes, there are similarities between public and private law enforcement.** But, there are also cases where the similarities "are different". (Read on for further clarification.)

PRIVATE LAW ENFORCEMENT OPPORTUNITIES

As previously stated, private law enforcement--otherwise known as private "security"-- is not a field comprised solely of guards or security officers. In fact, there are as many definitions of the field as there are practitioners and researchers *in* the field.

From Hess & Wrobleski (1996, pp. x-xi), **do any of the following private law enforcement-related occupational areas sound interesting to you?**

☑ **Industrial security** (security, sabotage, espionage, transporting goods);
☑ **Retail security** (shoplifting, bad checks, fraudulent credit cards, retail employee theft, shopping center/mall security);
☑ **Commercial security** (financial institution, office building, housing, hotel/motel, public gathering and special events, movie industry, recreational parks, racetracks, airport and airline, mass transit, cruise ship);
☑ **Institutional security** (hospitals and other health care facilities, educational, K-12, colleges and universities, libraries, museums and art galleries, religious facilities.

On the other hand, occupational areas can also be designated through a professional association. For example, the American Society for Industrial Security (ASIS) International represents over 32,000 security practitioners. Members can advertise under 33 distinctive categories in the ASIS International Job Bank Employment Resource Service (n.d.).

Do any of the following ASIS-based occupational areas sound interesting to you?

*Access control (50)	*Alarms (11)	*Bulletproofing (3)
*Business Continuity Planning (1)	*CCTV (42)	*Communications (12)
*Computer Security (15)	*Consulting (9)	*Counter-eavesdropping (6)
*Document Destruction (3)	*Education (5)	*Employee Screening (15)
*Emergency Communications (4)	*Fire Alarms (13)	*Guard Control (17)
*Identification Products (22)	*Insurance (6)	*Integrated Systems (32)
*Intrusion Detection (21)	*Investigation (4)	*Key Control (10)
*Locks and Safes (8)	*Newsletter (2)	*Perimeter Protection (18)
*Security Personnel (15)	*Glass (1)	*Guard Shelters (2)
*Software (18)	*Training (16)	*Uniforms/Accessories (1)
*Security Verification (4)	*Remote Videos (9)	*X-ray Screening (4)

COMPARISON OF PUBLIC & PRIVATE LAW ENFORCEMENT

Public and private law enforcement are not necessarily at war with each other. There are similarities and, then, "the similarities are different."

	PUBLIC LAW ENFORCEMENT	PRIVATE LAW ENFORCEMENT
1. MORE PEOPLE EMPLOYED?	No	2-½ times as many as public (Hess & Wrobleski, 1996, p. 57).
2. EMPLOYER?	Government agency	Private company and/or client
3. GOALS?	*Prevent crime *Crime control *Apprehend offenders	*Prevent crime *Protect assets (people, property, data, image) *Reduce losses (Hess & Wrobleski, 1996, p. 53).
4. CERTIFICATION AUTHORITY?	Yes: Ohio Peace Officer Training Council	Yes: Ohio Peace Officer Training Council
5. CERTIFICATION REQUIREMENTS?	555 hours of Basic Police Academy (see www.ag.state.oh.us)	157 hours of Private Security Training Academy (if carrying firearm)
6. LEGAL AUTHORITY?	Arrest, investigate, search and seizure, traffic enforcement, use of force per Ohio Revised Code, Ohio Administrative Code, Ohio & United States Constitution	*Arrest and investigate per citizen's arrest *Deny access to unauthorized personnel *Enforce employer's rules and regulations *Search employees *Use of force per law, in self-defense & if certified (Hess & Wrobleski, 1996, pp. 54-56).
7. CARRY WEAPONS?	Yes, if certified	Yes, if certified
8. OVERALL IMAGE OF FIELD?	Positive, especially since 9/11 terrorist attacks	Rarely receive the credit they so richly deserve.

WHAT ARE THE EMPLOYMENT NUMBERS?

In other words, will **you** be able to find employment in private law enforcement?

Consider the following *general* statistics from the *Occupational Outlook Handbook, 2002-2003,* (n.d.):

★ **"Security guards" is one of the top ten occupations with the largest job growth, 2002-2010!** It's eighth! (News release, Table 3c).

★ **Job opportunities exist now:** There are more than 1.1 million jobs (2000) for security officers in contractual, industrial firms and guard services (Security guards and gaming surveillance officers, Employment). Also, "(p)rivate detectives and investigators held about 39,000 jobs in 2000. About 2 out of 5 were self-employed. Approximately a third of salaried private detectives and investigators worked for detective agencies, while another third were employed as store detectives in department or clothing and accessories stores. The remainder worked for hotels and other lodging places, legal services firms, and in other industries" (Private detectives and investigators, Employment).

★ **Job opportunities in security will rise:** "Employment of security guards and gaming surveillance officers is expected to grow faster than the average for all occupations through 2010" (Security guards and gaming surveillance officers, Job Outlook, paragraph 2).

★ **Job opportunities in private investigations will rise:** "Employment of private detectives and investigators is expected to grow faster than the average for all occupations through 2010" (Private detectives and investigators, Job Outlook, paragraph 2).

★ **Educational requirements are minimal:** "Many employers of unarmed guards do not have any specific educational requirements. For armed guards, employers usually prefer individuals who are high school graduates..." (Security guards and gaming surveillance officers, Training, Other Qualifications, and Advancement). "There are no formal education requirements for most private detective and investigator jobs, although many private detectives have college degrees" (Private detective and investigators, Training, Other Qualifications, and Advancement).

45.

POSSIBLE EARNINGS IN PRIVATE LAW ENFORCEMENT

Still unsure whether private law enforcement is for you? **Consider the potential earnings for the private law enforcement field:**

☺ **"Median (most frequently occurring) annual earnings of security guards were $17,570 in 2000...(and) newly hired guards in the Federal Government earned $21,950 to $27,190 a year in 2001"** (Occupational Outlook Handbook, 2002-2003, n.d., Security guards and gaming surveillance officers, Earnings).

☺ **"Median annual earnings of salaried private detectives and investigators were $26,750 in 2000...the highest 10 percent earned more than $52,200** (Occupational Outlook Handbook, 2002-2003, n.d., Private detectives and investigators).

☺ **Thinking of promotions? Security managers (and consultants) earned an average of $70,812, in addition to health, dental and vision coverage, life insurance and 401K plan.** Also, according to The ASIS International 2001 Employment Survey (n.d., pp. xiv-xvi), security managers said they received performance bonuses (45% of survey respondents), profit sharing (18%), stock options and related benefits (16%). **WARNING!** There is a catch: the same survey indicated that in order to earn the money and benefits of a security manager and/or consultant, "...two-thirds hold a four-year college degree or higher. Of those with less than a four-year degree, 12 percent hold a two-year associate's degree and 15 percent have some four-year college experience" (p. xiv). Also, "most respondents (73%) are responsible for security at two or more locations within their organizations" (p. xv).

☺ **From an hourly compensation viewpoint (and The ASIS International 2001 Employment Survey (n.d., p. xvi):** Unarmed security officers earned $11-15 (proprietary) and $10-12 (contractually); conversely, armed security officers earned $13-18 (proprietary) and $16-23 (contractual). Investigators earned $23-32 (proprietary) and $45-62 (contractual).

A WORD ABOUT OHIO PRIVATE INVESTIGATORS

First, are you sure this field is for you? Circle the following statements which sound pertinent to your skills, knowledge, abilities and interests:

- I want to be a detective; but, don't want to be a police officer.
- I don't want to hold my breath, hoping a detective slot will open AND I'll get the job.
- I want to be a detective NOW, not after 2-3 years of service.
- I am good with computers and like doing computer-based research.
- I am willing to earn a 2-year, associate's degree. (Best for self-employment.)
- I am willing to earn a 4-year, bachelor's degree. (Best for corporate investigators.)
- I don't want a job where every day is the same.
- I don't want to work in a large company.
- I'd prefer to be a member of a team. ["Most private detective agencies are small, (without) defined ranks or steps, so advancement takes the form of increases in salary and assignment tasks" (*Occupational Outlook Handbook, 2002-2003,* n.d., Private detectives and investigators, Training, other qualifications, and advancement, paragraph 7).]
- I am willing to work different hours and on weekends.
- I don't mind sitting for long periods in a car or van, if I can conduct surveillance.
- I don't mind being outside in the rain, snow and sleet.
- I have good interpersonal communication skills.
- I can call people I don't know and obtain information over the phone.
- I am willing to be self-employed and research, service and protect my own clients.
- I am willing to get phone calls after hours and on weekends.
- I am interested in executive, corporate and celebrity protection.
- I am interested in investigating, documenting and giving testimony on such cases as "…civil liability and personal injury cases, insurance claims and fraud, child custody and protection cases, and premarital screening…(and) to prove or disprove infidelity" (*Occupational Outlook Handbook, 2002-2003,* n.d., Private detectives and investigators).
- I am organized and detail-oriented.
- I write logical, comprehensive reports.
- I can locate AND understand a document I wrote over a year ago.
- I have "…ingenuity, persistence and assertiveness…(and would) not be afraid of confrontation" (*Occupational Outlook Handbook, 2002-2003,* n.d. Private detectives and investigators, Training, other qualifications, and advancement, paragraph 4).

47.

PRIVATE INVESTIGATOR LICENSE IN OHIO

According to the Ohio Revised Code 4749.03, the licensing requirements for an Ohio private investigator are:

1) Good reputation for integrity;
2) Not convicted of a felony within the last 20 years or any offense involving moral turpitude;
3) Has not been adjudicated incompetent for the purpose of holding the license;
4) 2 years or more continuous experience as a lawyer or in investigatory or security services for public or private law enforcement, or experienced per Department of Commerce ruling. (In other words, earned a minimum of 4,000 hours experience OR 2,000 hours with associate's degree, per Ohio Administrative Code 1301:4-5-08 C, 1);
5) Pass Department of Commerce's examination for private investigator;
6) Prove you have insurance: $100,000 per person; $300,000 per occurrence re bodily injury liability; $100,000 for property damage liability;
7) Pay licensing fees.

CONCLUSION

After comparing public and private law enforcement, private law enforcement finished as a strong contender for career title, didn't it? Every business industry has a need to protect such valuable assets as employees, property, data and image. So, whatever your interests, there is a need--and job market--for a skilled, knowledgeable private law enforcement professional. Earnings and entry-level opportunities are more abundant than expected. Promotional opportunities, especially to security manager, are diverse, unlimited and lucrative. Furthermore, promotions are based on merit and performance, rather than the traditional standards for public law enforcement: seniority and departmental policy.

In the profit-oriented domain of private industry, your ability to consistently produce is valued and nurtured. Theoretically, a satisfied employee is a productive employee. To borrow a business world idiom: it's a win-win situation.

SUGGESTED READING

National Association of Legal Investigators at http://www.nalionline.org/

National Council of Investigation and Security Services at http://www.nciss.org/

Ohio Association of Security & Investigation Services (55 year old organization, currently listing 35 agencies and 127 members) at http://www.jhanda.com/oasis/

The Private Investigator's Mall at http://www.pimall.com/

REFERENCES

American Society for Industrial Security (ASIS) International. (n.d.). *The ASIS International 2001 employment survey: Not all security compensation is created equal--Where are* You *on the salary continuum?* Retrieved September 14, 2002, from http://www.sibgonline.com/public/PDFs/ASIS_Employ_Survey_01.pdf

American Society for Industrial Security (ASIS) International. (n.d.). *Job bank employment resource service.* Retrieved September 14, 2002, from http://www.asisonline.org/ers.html

American Society for Industrial Security (ASIS) International. (n.d.). *Security management* - Advertisers by category. Retrieved September 14, 2002, from http://www.securitymanagement.com/ads/bycategory.html

Hess, K. M., & Wrobleski, H. M. (1996). *Introduction to Private Security.* St. Paul, MN: West Publishing Company.

Occupational Outlook Handbook, 2002-2003. (n.d.). *News release, table 3c: Occupations with the largest job growth, 2000-2010.* Retrieved September 1, 2002, from http://www.bls.gov/news.release/ecopro.t07.htm

Occupational Outlook Handbook, 2002-2003. (n.d.). *Security guards and gaming surveillance officers.* Retrieved September 1, 2002, from http://www.bls.gov/oco/ocos159.htm

Occupational Outlook Handbook, 2002-2003. (n.d.). *Private detectives and investigators.* Retrieved September 14, 2002, from http://www.bls.gov/oco/ocos157.htm

Ohio Administrative Code. (n.d.) *Anderson Publishing Company's On-line Documents: Chapter 1301: 4-5 Private Investigation; OAC 1301: 4-5-08 C, 1.* Retrieved September 14, 2002, from http://onlinedocs.andersonpublishing.com/oac/

Ohio Revised Code. (n.d.). *Anderson Publishing Company's On-line Documents; Chapter 4749: Private Investigators; Security Services; ORC 4749.03.* Retrieved September 14, 2002, from http://onlinedocs.andersonpublishing.com/revisedcode/

CHAPTER 5

LOOKING AT OHIO LAW ENFORCEMENT TESTING

"Destiny is not a matter of chance,
it is a matter of choice;
it is not a thing to be waited for,
it is a thing to be achieved."
-William Jennings Bryan

AFTER READING THIS CHAPTER, YOU SHOULD KNOW
⇨ The standard procedures for police testing.
⇨ What are the elimination factors for policing.
⇨ What is entailed in testing knowledge.
⇨ The physical fitness standards for Ohio law enforcement.
⇨ What procedures are followed for psychological tests.
⇨ Whether polygraph testing is required.
⇨ What questions can be asked in an oral interview.
⇨ How a personal history investigation is conducted.
⇨ Whether a medical examination is legal.
⇨ How go you get accepted into Ohio's Basic Police Academy.

INTRODUCTION

You investigated your occupational preferences for public employment at the municipal, county, regional, state or federal levels (Chapter 3) and analyzed the wide spectrum of employment and promotional opportunities in private law enforcement (Chapter 4). But, *how* do you attain that coveted law enforcement position, and what can exclude you from applying? What testing procedures are involved in the hiring process? Which tests can you prepare for now, before entering Ohio's Basic Police Academy? What's entailed in Ohio's Basic Police Academy and *how* do you get into the Academy in the first place?

In this chapter, the testing procedures for a police position will be examined by comparing six major sources: Cincinnati, Cleveland, Columbus, Dayton, Ohio State Highway Patrol and, when applicable, the Ohio Basic Police Academy. (We encourage you to visit the pertinent website for additional exploration of standards.)

"STANDARD" TESTING IN OHIO

Why do we need a separate section explaining "standard" police testing in Ohio? Because, while legal standards are consistently applied across Ohio, the actual tests conducted (frequently called, testing instruments) vary from department to department.

Testing standards are based on:

★ **State and Federally legislated acts.** Because of the scope and depth of employment law, the subject is more comprehensively addressed in Chapter 10.

★ **Industry standards.** These standards are considered "industry"-related because they are frequently utilized by public law enforcement agencies across America and/or Ohio. They are considered standards since they have been valid and reliable through duplication, withstood grievances or litigation complaints and are understood by the key decision-makers in the hiring process. For example, while the psychological testing/assessment phase in the hiring process could be completed through any number of testing instruments, an agency may favor one particular test because of its traditional history in law enforcement testing.

★ **Civil litigation decisions.** For example, "based on the Federal Court Consent Decree for the Cincinnati Police Department, the recruit class will be 34% Black and 23% female" (Cincinnati Police Department, n.d., *City of Cincinnati exam information guide for police recruit 2002-2003* (website), p. 7).

★ **Research conducted or preferred by the agency.** The Ohio Peace Officer Basic Training Program's Physical Fitness (exit) Standards are based on Cooper Institute for Aerobics Research, national norms (Ohio Peace Officer Training Academy, n.d., Fitness standards).

★ **Tradition, otherwise known as the "if-it-ain't broke, don't-fix-it" philosophy.** No litigation? No grievances? Works for us? The Chief or Sheriff likes this test? Then, keep it in the hiring process.

★ **Civil suit precedents.** Every agency must be protected against an unsuitable candidate and/or negligent hiring civil suit. Therefore, the agency usually proceeds in a comprehensive, cautious, time intensive manner. Columbus Police Department (n.d.) notes the hiring process could take 4 to 12 months; but, as a rough rule, figure approximately one month per step in the hiring, pre-employment screening process.

ELIMINATION FACTORS

"Skeletons in the closet" *can* hurt you in policing. **Could any of these non-physical fitness factors eliminate you for the policing field?**

POLICE DEPARTMENT	FACTORS WHICH MAY ELIMINATE AN APPLICANT	SUGGESTION: VISIT THEIR WEBSITE
1. CINCINNATI	-Felony conviction. -Misdemeanor within 5 years. -2 job-related Misdemeanor convictions. -Controlled substance/Marijuana offense. -Sex or Bodily Harm offense. -Weapons/dangerous ordinance offense. -Serious driving conviction in 5 years, 2+ DUS or 6+ points on current record.	http://www.cincinnati police.org/pdf/prguide. pdf
2. CLEVELAND	-Not meet entry-level qualifications. -No other details given.	http://www.cleveland pd.net/recruit.htm
3. COLUMBUS	-Not meet entry-level qualifications. -No other details given.	http://www.columbus police.org/Employ ment/RECRUIT.HTM
4. DAYTON	-Felony conviction. -Misdemeanor conviction. -Controlled substance offense within 8 years or after 25 years of age. -Repeated conviction of an offense. -"Poor" credit record. -Repeated discharge from employment. -Exhibiting "deviant" behavior traits. -Military discharge other than honorable. -Good driving history.	http://www.cityof dayton.org/police/ Dayton%20Police% 20Department%20 Recruitment.asp
5. OHIO STATE PATROL	-Felony conviction or conduct. -Non-compliance with law. -Illegal use (or conviction) re drugs. -Intemperate use of alcohol. -Anti-social behavior. -Poor work record -Poor driving record.	http://www.state.oh. us/ohiostatepatrol/ office/recruit/ applican.html

TESTING KNOWLEDGE OR WRITTEN EXAMINATIONS

As the first step in the hiring process, a high score is crucial! Have you practiced for this written examination?

- ☑ Cincinnati Police Department's website offers samples of test questions;
- ◎ Target communication skills by reviewing college entrance manuals (ACT, SAT) ;
- ✹ "Bomb" on memory tests? Study a picture or scene for 1 minute; look away; describe the scene. Be sure to note location, sequence, color of items. How did you do? Need to improve? Practice makes perfect!

How would YOU do on the following knowledge-based, testing procedures?

POLICE DEPARTMENT	AREAS ON WRITTEN EXAM
1. CINCINNATI http://www.cincinnati police.org/pdf/prguide.pdf	*Human relations *Following Directions *Reasoning *Reading comprehension *Observation and memory *Basic math *Evaluating situations/decision-making *Dealing effectively with a diverse group of people *Oral/written communication (words, spelling, grammar)
2. CLEVELAND http://www.cleveland pd.net/recruit.htm	*No details given.
3. COLUMBUS http://www.columbus police.org/Employ ment/RECRUIT.HTM	*Multiple choice examination (Pass/Fail) *Writing sample (Pass/Fail)
4. DAYTON http://www.cityof dayton.org/police/ Dayton%20Police% 20Department%20 Recruitment.asp	*Must pass written examination with 70% or higher. *No additional details given.
5. OHIO STATE PATROL http://www.state.oh. us/ohiostatepatrol/ office/recruit/ applican.html	Three-part test: *Decision-making skills; *Ability to read and comprehend information; *Ability to use information.

PHYSICAL FITNESS STANDARDS

Well! This is certainly more difficult to explain than you'd think! The Ohio Attorney General oversees O.P.O.T.C. or the Ohio Peace Officer Training Commission, which mandates procedural, academic, behavioral, and fitness standards for any authorized Ohio Peace Officer Training Academy (otherwise known as the Basic Police Academy). **So, in order to successfully complete the Basic Police Academy, all law enforcement candidates must pass O.P.O.T.C. Physical Fitness standards:**

AGE*	MALE	FEMALE
UNDER 29	40 Sit-ups (1 minute) 33 Push-ups 1.5 mile run (12:18 minutes)	35 Sit-ups (1 minute) 18 Push-ups 1.5 mile run (14:55 minutes)
30-39 YEARS	36 Sit-ups (1 minutes) 27 Push-ups 1.5 mile run (12:51 minutes)	27 Sit-ups (1 minute) 13 Push-ups 1.5 mile run (15:26 minutes)

*For anyone aged 40 or over, visit the Ohio Peace Officer Basic Training Program Physical Fitness Standards at http://www.ag.state.oh.us/opota/forms.htm

BUT, each law enforcement department can set physical fitness standards for hiring the officer, as long as the standards are job-related and do not conflict with state mandates. **So, could you pass these departmental physical fitness standards?**

POLICE DEPARTMENT	PHYSICAL FITNESS STANDARDS
1. CINCINNATI http://www.cincinnatipolice.org/pdf/ prguide.pdf (NOTE: This website includes suggestions for warm-ups, exercises and rationales for each step of their obstacle course.)	**Obstacle Course, wearing 11 pound weight belt AND 5 pound body armor:** **+Run 2.5 times around perimeter;** **+Complete obstacle course** (6 minutes, including running, sprints, negotiating cones, fence climb, jumping a "culvert", barricade climb, climb through a window, dummy drag and dry fire a weapon. **+Run 2.5 times around perimeter.**

POLICE DEPARTMENT (CONTINUED)	PHYSICAL FITNESS STANDARDS (CONTINUED)
2. CLEVELAND http://www.cleveland pd.net/recruit.htm	*No details given
3. COLUMBUS http://www.columbuspolice.org/ Employ ment/RECRUIT.HTM	**Obstacle (60 yard) Course (21 seconds);** **Bench press (70% body weight);** **Vertical jump; 300 meter run (70 sec.);** **23 push-ups; 31 sit-ups; 1.5 mile run** **(17:53 minutes).**
4. DAYTON http://www.cityof dayton.org/police/ Dayton%20Police% 20Department%20 Recruitment.asp	No details given regarding pre-hire testing. State must pass testing prior to end of Academy training.

5. OHIO STATE
    PATROL
http://www.state.oh. us/ohiostatepatrol/
office/recruit/ applican.html
	30% for candidate's age and gender re:
	+Body fat; Bench press; Leg press;
	    Flexibility; VO$_2$; Endurance Test (1.5 mile
	    run); Grip strength.
	Anyone interested in OSP is
	STRONGLY urged to review the fitness
	details on the website, especially
	regarding grip strength.

PSYCHOLOGICAL TESTING

Do any of the following statements sound like *you*?
1. I don't know what to expect from this test.
2. I don't understand why I have to take this test.
3. I don't know what they're looking for, anyway.
4. I don't know what I should say…or leave out.
5. I thought these tests weren't accurate.
6. How can I study for these tests?

Let's take these questions, one at a time:

1. **I don't know what to expect from this test.** Surprisingly, this is one of the hardest statements to address because testing varies from agency to agency. This testing step

may occur after the written examination or be scheduled for the end of the process. Cincinnati Police Department's City of Cincinnati Exam Information Guide for Police Recruit 2002-2003 (n.d.) does not identify their step as a "psychological exam" but as "a behavior assessment". Then, Cleveland Police Department's recruitment website (n.d.) does not list one test but two: "…(a) Psychological/psychiatric examination…(and a) Psychological/psychiatric evaluation."

2. **I don't understand why I have to take this test.** McCoy & Skonecki (2001, p. 179) respond by stating "…it is clear that agency administrators recognize a need to reduce the potential liability incurred by the selection of a person who may be emotionally unstable or be a high risk to an agency."

3. **I don't know what they're looking for, anyway.** The tests, themselves, vary in nature and scope. Harr & Hess (2003, p. 113) distinquish the scope of ten standard psychological exams utilized by the criminal justice field. The nature of the tests concern either a personality tests ("Do you prefer to go out to a party or stay home with close friends?") or projective ("What images do you see in this inkblot?") Harr & Hess (2003, p. 114) identify the Minnesota Multiphasic Personality Inventory (MMPI) as "…the most widely used paper-and-pencil personality test being used (in all fields)…covering…(a wide scope of topics, such as) health, social, political, sexual and religious values; attitudes about family, education and occupation; emotional moods; and typical neurotic or psychotic displays…."

4. **I don't know what I should say…or leave out.** Be honest. Psychological tests probably have validity and reliability measurements built into their test: they ask the same question or address the same issue more than once. If there is a deviation between answers, the validity or "truthfulness) of your answer is suspect because your answer wasn't reliable.

5. **I thought these tests weren't accurate.** On the contrary, these tests are "accurate" or litigious-minded applicants would have eradicated the tests from the criminal justice hiring process. Besides, if these tests were *not* accurate, how could the Ohio State Patrol continue to require a *four hour* psychological assessment? (See http://www.state.oh.us/ohiostatepatrol/office/recruit/applican.html for details.)

6. **How can I study for these tests?** Trick question. You can't *study* for these tests because they measure *you*! However, any behavior which personally assists *you* in coping with stress will also assist you in being better prepared to do your best during the psychological testing. Since "…psychological testing disqualified 40 to 60 percent of applicants" (Harr & Hess, 2003, p. 113) managing *your* stress-levels before and during the exam is critical. When pressed for a practical suggestion, the most effective advice for addressing a written psychological test is to pretend you are severely limited for time: you are less likely to project *your* interpretation into *their* test and more likely to be consistent in your answers if you don't overanalyze or dwell on an answer.

POLYGRAPH TESTING

Answer the following questions as True or False:

_____ 1.   Polygraphs measure only blood pressure and pulse rate.

_____ 2.   The United States Supreme Court considers polygraph evidence reliable.

_____ 3.   Polygraph examiners say polygraphs are reliable.

_____ 4.   Polygraphs cannot be used for pre-employment screenings.

_____ 5.   Computerized polygraphs are considered more reliable than traditional, mechanical polygraphs.

_____ 6.   You can "beat" a polygraph.

_____ 7.   You can appeal if you "fail" a polygraph.

_____ 8.   Nothing will happen to you if you are caught "lying" on a polygraph.

How did you do?

☹ **FALSE**   1.   Polygraphs measure blood pressure, pulse rate, perspiration (galvanic skin resistance/GSR), and both stomach and chest breathing patterns.

☯ **TRICKY!** 2.   The United States Supreme Court considers polygraph evidence reliable enough to be used in court if both parties stipulate to its use. However, "…the (United States) Supreme Court has held there is simply no consensus that polygraph evidence is reliable" (Harr & Hess, 2003, p. 116).

☺ **TRUE**   3.   Polygraph examiners say polygraphs **are** 90 to 95 percent reliable (Harr & Hess, 2003, p. 116).

☯ **TRICKY!** 4.   Polygraphs **can** be used for pre-employment screenings, **but only** if the employer is in the private industry or local, state or Federal government (Harr & Hess, 2003, p. 116).

☺ **TRUE**   5.   Computerized polygraphs are considered over 95 percent reliable.

◎ **FALSE!** 6.   A skilled practitioner will be on the target, able to observe and/or record your less-than-truthful answers.

☎ **TRICKY!** 7.   You *may* be able to appeal if you "fail" a polygraph: it depends on the agency's civil service standards and operating procedures. You'd have to call the agency *if and when* you fail the polygraph: no need to criticize nor telegraph your concerns about the prospective employer's screening procedures. However, the stigma of having failed the polygraph will probably linger, making an appeal superfluous.

💣 **FALSE!** 8.   Falsifying any information during any stage of the process is usually grounds for elimination from the hiring process. If the falsification or deception is discovered *after* you're hired, the employer will probably terminate the deceiving employee.

ORAL INTERVIEW

Interviews are an intense, complex and critical stage of the pre-employment screening process. Consequently, interview procedures, frequently asked questions and suggested responses are more comprehensively addressed in Chapter 12: "Interesting Interviews". However, we thought it best to discuss lawful and unlawful questions (and appropriate responses to unlawful questions) under Chapter 10: "Legal Liabilities".

BACKGROUND CHECK

A background check puts your personal history under a microscope. In other words, the prospective employers reviews all the information you wrote in your job application and resume. Neighbors, relatives, supervisors, co-workers, relatives may be interviewed.

The background investigator may even visit and interview you at your home!
Could YOU pass a rigorous investigation into these aspects of your life?

FACTORS TO INVESTIGATE	WHY IS THIS A CONCERN?	CORRECTIVE MEASURES?
1. **CRIMINAL HISTORY**	*Daily temptations *Corrupting influences *Negligent hiring ("with the candidate's history, shouldn't you have know s/he would do that?")	◎ Don't lie. Practice answering 3 questions: 1) Can you take responsibility for your actions? 2) Have you learned from your mistakes? 3) Are you taking pre-cautions not to repeat past mistakes?
2. **TRAFFIC RECORD HISTORY**	*Driving in foul weather *High speed pursuits *Ability to get/retain insurance coverage *Negligent hiring	✂ Cut out speeding. ☑ If violations, be prepared to answer above 3 questions.
3. **EMPLOY-MENT GAPS**	*Poor employment history *In jail or prison *Hints of poor work ethic	☺ Be pro-active if 3+ month gap: explain on job application i.e. laid off; seasonal; summer while not in school; moved.
4. **EMPLOY-MENT HISTORY**	*Inability to work with diverse people *Disciplinary problems *Absenteeism/Tardiness	◎ Target diverse work experience on resume. ☺ Try to get along with fellow employees. ✂ Tardiness, absenteeism. ☑ Maintain exemplary work record.
5. **REASONS FOR LEAVING A JOB**	*Inconsistent work ethic *Lack of employer-loyalty *Worry not give advance notice	☺ Show stability & responsibility. ☻ Would employer re-hire candidate? ☞ Give 2 weeks advance notice, offer to train re-placement employee.
6. **EDUCA-TIONAL HISTORY**	*Proof of education *Grade point average/IQ *Extracurricular activities	★ Attach photocopy of transcripts. ☻ Take fewer classes to improve grades. ◎ Target clubs, associations, honor societies.
7. **MILITARY SERVICE**	*Verify in-service dates *Verify dates out of service *Rank & training issues	☑ Maintain stellar military work history. ☹ Don't have brig/jail time. ☞ Take advantage of classes & promotions.
8. **FAMILY HISTORY**	*Lack of family support *Personal habits & lifestyle	★ Explain work goals to family. ★ Obtain support of family members.
9. **NEIGH-BORS**	*Unusual/inappropriate Behaviors or lifestyle	☑ Have positive relationship with neighbors. ✂ Cut out parties/disruptive behavior.
10. **IN-HOME INTERVIEW**	*Personal habits *Lifestyle	☑ Maintain exterior and interior of home for unannounced visit.

MEDICAL EXAMINATION

Let's be pro-active and answer the most frequently asked questions concerning a medical examination:

1. **Yes, a medical examination is legal.** "The Americans with Disabilities Act (ADA) prohibits medical examinations or inquiries regarding mental or physical problems or disabilities *before* a conditional offer of employment" (Harr & Hess, 2003, p. 94). Otherwise, the medical examination is illegal.

2. **Yes, employers consider the medical exam a necessity.** The exam reduces the likelihood of absenteeism and medical insurance costs. Healthy employees also reduce the probability of having to hiring, training and equip personnel who have replaced disabled or unhealthy employees.

3. **No, you don't have to pay for the exam.** If it's required as a condition of employment, the employer pays. If you are appealing a medical diagnosis, however, you will have to pay for your own exam, by your own physician.

4. **Yes, you have to take the medical exam…unless you don't want the job.**

5. **No, the medical examination cannot be invasive.** Basically, remember your last annual physical. Both the Columbus Police Department (n.d.) and Ohio State Patrol (n.d.) eliminate for color blindness and require vision acuity of no more than 20/125 binocular uncorrected, 20/20 corrected. The exam may also include checks regarding hearing; cardiovascular-respiratory system; blood pressure; smoking/drug use; blood sugar level; cholesterol (Harr & Hess, 2003, p. 94).

6. **Yes, "(t)he medical examination must be job related and verifiable"** (Lieske, 2001, p. 197).

7. **Yes, "(d)rug screening of candidates is legal as long as it is done uniformly and consistent…"** (Lieske, 2001, p. 195).

8. **Yes, the exam can screen for disabilities, including those related to Worker's Compensation.** But, the screening must occur after conditional offer of employment. Also, "(i)f a medical examination screens out an individual with a disability, the employer must be able to demonstrate that the rejection is job related and consistent with the job" (Lieske, 2001, p. 197).

OHIO'S BASIC POLICE ACADEMY

Now, you're facing the Ohio Peace Officer Basic Training Academy, commonly referred to as the "Basic Police Academy". But, what is the Academy and how do you get in one?

Facts about Ohio's Peace Officer Basic Training Academy (Police Academy):

1. **There are 69 different Ohio Academies.** (For a listing of all available academies, visit Ohio Peace Officer Training Academy, n.d., Directory of peace officer basic training academies in Ohio at http://www.ag.state.oh.us/opota/downloads/Directory-Cmdr.PDF)

2. **The curriculum must include the state-mandated, 550-hour curriculum of over 100 subjects** (Ohio Peace Officer Training Academy, n.d., Directory of peace officer basic training academies in Ohio.) However, the hosting academy can add curriculum, if approved by the Ohio Peace Officer Training Council. In other words, an academy can be more than 550 hours, but not less.

3. **You can enter the academy as either "a commissioned officer":**
    ☺ You have already been hired by an authorized Ohio law enforcement agency.
    ☺ You have taken the "oath of office".
    ★ The agency pays for your academy.
    ★ The agency pays you a salary while completing the academy.
    ★ You can attend 59 of the 69 academies. See http://www.ag.state.oh.us/opota/downloads/Directory-Cmdr.PDF
    ☹ The salary is usually at a diminished wage because, after all, they are paying you to be an officer, without your having the ability to do law enforcement.
    ☻ But, the salary must be a "living" wage…you'll probably be able to pay reasonable living expenses, just don't expect to live well.
    ☀ These opportunities are limited: they're costly for the agency and the agency does not have to pay to get candidates. Many candidates are more than willing to pay for the academy and get a side-job, just for the chance of getting hired.

4. **On the other hand, you can enter the academy under "open enrollment":**
    ☹ You have *not* been hired by an agency nor taken the "oath of office".
    ☹ You must pay for your own academy.
    ☹ You do not earn a salary unless you are already employed.
    ★ You can attend 50 of the 69 academies. See http://www.ag.state.oh.us/opota/downloads/Directory-Cmdr.PDF
    ☹ Seating may be limited in each academy: preference is for commissioned officers.

5. **There are 3 kinds of Academies: academies, college academies and Department's (own) commissioned officers-style academies.**
   - ◎ **"Academies"** are more regional and usually accept both open enrollment and commissioned officers. There are 60 such academies that are not limited to either a 2-year college nor individual department. Most open enrollment candidates attend one of these academies.

   - ◎ **"Departmental academies"** are when an agency runs its own academy.
     - ★ **One type, no "official" name for this kind of departmental academy :** the department sponsors its own academy but allows other department's commissioned officers to attend. There are 35 such academies in Ohio.
     - ★ **Second type, no "official" name for this departmental academy:** even if you have previously and successfully completed an Ohio Peace Officer Basic Training Academy, you will still be required to go through this type of academy, all over again. There are 6 such academies: Akron, Cincinnati, Cleveland, Columbus, Dayton Police Departments; Ohio State Highway Patrol; and Wood County Sheriff's Academy.

   - ◎ **"College academies"** are based at 2-year community colleges. All 6 of these academies accept their own commissioned officers, other department's commissioned officers and open enrollment students. These academies may run concurrently with an associate's degree in applied science, such as law enforcement. Despite being based in a college setting, they are each a state-certified Peace Officer Basic Training Academy.

6. **The length of police academies vary.** For instance, the Ohio Highway Patrol's Academy (n.d.) is 18 weeks, the Cleveland Police Department's Academy (n.d.) is 19 weeks, while the Columbus Police Department's Academy (n.d.) is 28 weeks in length.

7. **While attending the academy, consider your life "on hold":**
   - ● The academy is your last obstacle to becoming a police officer: don't under-estimate its importance to your career.
   - ★ Your academy instructors will be respected officers in the field who could easily recommend or eliminate you from the hiring pool. Work as hard as you can to make a good impression: even if your instructor doesn't have authority to hire you, your instructor may be willing to be a job reference for you!
   - ☺ Many academies are daytime, Monday through Friday.
   - ☹ However, there will be night and weekend classes.
   - ♫ Grades and scores will be kept and homework will be due.
   - ● There are mandatory classes you cannot miss, despite serious illness, marriages, deaths in the family, appearances in court. If you miss a mandatory class, unless the rare exception is made by the Ohio Peace Officer Training Council, you are out of the academy--even if the missed mandatory class is the last day of class!

8. Ranking in the academy *does* matter!
- 💣 Why should a chief hire the last in the class, when the chief can hire the first?
- 😞 Think of the liability and media fiasco if word leaked that the chief hired the officer ranked in the *bottom* 10 percent of the class, not the *top* 10 percent!
- 💣 Would *you* want a backup who was ranked at the bottom of the class?

CONCLUSION

In this chapter, you have discovered factors in your personal history which could eliminate you from policing, before you've even begun your career! Comparing and contrasting 5 major departments in Ohio, the requirements for 6 hiring tests or pre-employment screening stages were examined: the written exam; physical fitness; psychological; polygraph; background; and medical. The complex issue of Ohio's Peace Officer Basic Training Academy (Basic Police Academy) was addressed and included such varied topics as overall structure, length, jurisdiction, location, availability and suggestions for success. However, as was also noted in this chapter, employment law is too complex to be a footnote in the hiring process and will be closely examined in Chapter 10's "The Hiring Process". Also, recommended preparation, behaviors and answers concerning the oral interview will be comprehensively addressed in Chapter 12's "Interesting Interviews".

SUGGESTED READING

Cincinnati Police Department; Cincinnati, Ohio at http://www.cincinnatipolice.org/ pdf/prguide.pdf

Cleveland Police Department; Cleveland, Ohio at http://www.clevelandpd.net/recruit.htm

Columbus Police Department; Columbus, Ohio at http://www.columbuspolice.org/ Employment/RECRUIT.HTM

Dayton Police Department; Dayton, Ohio at http://www.cityofdayton.org/police/ Dayton%20Police%20Department%20Recruitment.asp

Ohio Peace Officer Training Academy, (by) County Listing of Peace Officer Basic Training Academies and 2-year College Academies at http://www.ag.state.oh.us/ opota/downloads/Directory-Cmdr.PDF)

Ohio State Highway Patrol; London, Ohio at http://www.state.oh.us/ohiostatepatrol/
Office/recruit/applican.html

REFERENCES

Attorney General of Ohio. (n.d.). *Ohio peace officer basic training program physical fitness (exit) standards; Ohio peace officer training academy; and Directory of peace officer basic training academies in Ohio.* Retrieved October 4, 2002, from http://www.ag.state.oh.us/opota

Cincinnati Police Department; Cincinnati, Ohio. (n.d.). *City of Cincinnati exam information guide for police recruit 2002-2003.* Retrieved October 4, 2002, from http://www.cincinnatipolice.org/pdf/prguide.pdf

Cleveland Police Department; Cleveland, Ohio. (n.d.). *Consider a career in law enforcement.* Retrieved October 4, 2002, from http://www.clevelandpd.net/recruit.htm

Columbus Police Department; Columbus, Ohio. (n.d.). *Employment Information.* Retrieved October 4, 2002, from http://www.columbuspolice.org/Employment/RECRUIT.HTM

Dayton Police Department; Dayton, Ohio. (n.d.). *Recruitment.* Retrieved October 4, 2002, from http://www.cityofdayton.org/police/Dayton%20Police%20Department%20Recruitment.asp

Harr, J. S. & Hess, K. M. (2003). *Seeking employment in criminal justice and related fields.* Belmont, CA: Wadsworth/Thomson Learning.

Lieske, Chief K. (2001). Medical examination. In *The complete guide to hiring law enforcement officers* (pp. 187-197). Columbus, OH; Law Enforcement Foundation, Inc.

McCoy, Chief W. & Skonecki, Chief J. (2001). Psychological examination. In *The complete guide to hiring law enforcement officers* (pp. 177-185). Columbus, OH: Law Enforcement Foundation, Inc.

Ohio State Highway Patrol; London, Ohio. (n.d.) *Ohio Trooper applicant process.* Retrieved October 4, 2002 from http://www.state.oh.us/ohiostatepatrol/office/recruit/applican.html

CHAPTER 6

COVERING CORRECTIONS CAREERS

"Trying a man is easy, as easy as falling off a log, compared with deciding what to do with him when he has been found guilty."
-Sir Henry Alfred McCardie

AFTER READING THIS CHAPTER, YOU SHOULD KNOW
- ⇨ What are the early methods of dealing with criminal populations.
- ⇨ Why the early methods of dealing with criminal populations are important to a modern career in corrections.
- ⇨ What are the correctional employment numbers.
- ⇨ How jails and prisons compare.
- ⇨ How probation and parole compare.
- ⇨ What local and county corrections opportunities exist.
- ⇨ What a CBCF is and how it impact career opportunities.
- ⇨ What correctional opportunities exist in Ohio.
- ⇨ The structure of and opportunities with the ODRC/Ohio Department of Rehabilitation and Corrections.
- ⇨ What parole opportunities exist through the State of Ohio.
- ⇨ How federal correctional agencies are organized.
- ⇨ What salary and benefits exist for those employed in federal-level corrections.

INTRODUCTION

So, what is meant by the term "corrections"? Are there other jobs and careers in corrections at all levels or only at the federal-level? How do jails and prisons compare and contrast? Are programs like boot camps considered part of the correctional field? What does a probation officer do? Don't they have the same authority and responsibilities as parole officers? Would I be better suited for a career at the county level? What's the difference between state and federal corrections?

All excellent questions! But, with such a monumental task of defining the correctional field and associated career opportunities, where should we start? Let's start at the beginning....

ONCE UPON A TIME IN CORRECTIONAL HISTORY

The key to any well-written story is the foundation: the beginning. The field of corrections is no different. To know the history of corrections is important to understanding the philosophies, definitions and opportunities in the modern field of corrections. **So, let's test your Correctional History IQ, True or False:**

_____ 1. The concept of imprisonment for crimes committed is relatively new to society.

_____ 2. The extensive use of corporal punishment (branding, dismemberment, flogging, etc…) was rarely used for punishing criminals.

_____ 3. The workhouse movement believed in convicted criminals performing day labor and being confined at night.

_____ 4. The workhouse movement has only British origins.

_____ 5. After the founding of America, the Pennsylvania Quakers used hard labor as a catalyst for individual reform.

_____ 6. By the mid-19th century, reform-minded administrators began promoting the reformatory movement (individualized treatment, education and vocational training).

_____ 7. The rehabilitation model emerged from houses of corrections, penitentiaries and reformatories.

_____ 8. Rehabilitation emphasized crime control and determinate sentencing (definite, set number of years).

_____ 9. Since 1980's, the correctional field has moved toward official retribution or the just-deserts model, where the criminal gets "just" what s/he "deserves".

_____ 10. The modern correctional institution followed the just desert model of the 1980's.

So, how did you do? Answers to Correctional History IQ Quiz:

TRUE! 1.   Before the 1700's, confinement didn't exist because "English courts… imposed one of two sanctions on convicted felons: they turned them loose or they executed them" (Gaines, L. K., Kaune, M., & Miller, R. L., 2001, p. 310).

FALSE! 2.   Corporal punishment (branding, dismemberment, flogging, etc…) was not only used but preferred "…well into the 19th century" (Cole, G. F., & Smith, C. E., 1999, p. 255).

TRUE! 3.   If the criminal couldn't pay restitution, s/he would "work-off" the fine by day and be confined at night (Gaines, L. K., Kaune, M., & Miller, R. L., 2001, p. 311.) Yes, we **still** have **financial** restitution (fines) and **restitution-in-kind,** the ability to work to pay off a court-imposed fine.

TRICKY! 4.   The workhouse movement was strongly influenced by British origins but championed by an *American:* Pennsylvania Quaker, William Penn in 1682 (Gaines, L. K., Kaune, M. & Miller, R. L., 2001, p. 311).

TRUE! 5.   Hard labor, reading the bible, and being "penitent" helped the Quakers found "penitentiaries". (See history impacts modern life!)

TRUE! 6.   Of course! (We took pity on you and "gave you one".)

TRUE! 7.   Penitentiaries had failed: they were "…overcrowded, understaffed, minimally financed, discipline was lax, brutality was common, and administrators were viewed as corrupt" (Cole, G. F., & Smith, C. E., 1999, p. 258). Again, sounds similar to "modern" institutions, doesn't it?

FALSE! 8.   Rehabilitation emphasizes "the need to restore a convicted offender to a constructive place in society through…training or therapy" (Cole, G. F., & Smith, C. E., 1999, p. 260) and supports indeterminate sentencing (Cole, G. F., & Smith, C. E., 1999, p. 230). **Determinate** sentencing means no matter how well you do, you still get the same fixed sentence as if you'd been rotten. **But, an indeterminate** sentence is determined by your own behavior: do the training and therapy, get released in less time. With such an incentive, why wouldn't you at least try to act rehabilitated?

TRUE! 9.   "The number of Americans in prison or jail has doubled since 1985 and continues to rise at an annual rate of between 5 and 7 percent" (Gaines, L. K., Kaune, M., & Miller, R. L., 2001, p. 314.)

TRUE! 10.   Common sense and another easy one to help you finish the quiz.

68.

WHAT ARE THE EMPLOYMENT NUMBERS?

Consider the following *general* statistics from the *Occupational Outlook Handbook, 2002-2003*, (12-31-01, *News releases)* and our Chapter 3:

★ **Service-producing occupations will remain the dominant employment,** generating 20.5 million jobs by 2010 (2000-2010 Employment projections).

★ **Service occupations will rise:** 19.5 percent between the years 2000 and 2010 (table 2) or 1.8 percent each year (table 1).

★ **Retirements are pending:** resulting in job openings!

Specifically, according to the *Occupational Outlook Handbook, 2002-2003,* n.d.:

★ "Employment for correctional officers is expected to grow faster than the average for all occupations through 2010" (**both** Corrections officer **and** Probation officers and correctional treatment specialists, Job Outlook Section, paragraph 2).

★ "...(V)igorous law enforcement is expected to result in a continuing increase in the prison population" (Probation officers and correctional treatment specialists, Job Outlook Section, paragraph 1).

★ "Correctional officers held about 457,000 jobs in 2000. About 60 percent were employed in State correctional institutions such as prisons, prison camps, and youth correctional facilities. Others were employed at the city and county level. About 15,000 were employed in federal facilities and about 19,000 were employed in privately owned and managed prisons" (Correctional officers, Employment).

JAILS VS. PRISONS

So, what's the big deal? A correctional facility is a correctional facility, right? Wrong.

How about another quiz. Do these statements apply to Jails, Prisons or Both?

_____ 1. Confines convicted misdemeanants, those service a sentence of one year or less.

_____ 2. Confines convicted felons, those serving a sentence of one year or more.

_____ 3. Under control of the Federal Bureau of Prisons.

_____ 4. Under control of the Ohio Department of Rehabilitation and Corrections.

_____ 5. Classifies inmates under 4 levels of security risks: minimum, medium, maximum, supermax/administrative.

_____ 6. Can be administered by the county sheriff.

_____ 7. Receives a "surprise" visit by each Grand Jury re institutional and inmate conditions and safety.

_____ 8. Has treatment programs, such as psychological treatment, chemical abuse, anger management, etc....

_____ 9. Provides G.E.D./high school equivalency classes.

_____ 10. Provides vocational training programs.

How did you do? Answers to Jails vs. Prisons Quiz:

JAILS 1. Could confines convicted misdemeanants for: crimes; contempt of court; mental illness; witness protection; pretrial detainees (couldn't get or pay bail); anyone awaiting transportation to another facility (probation and parole violators, military personnel, bail-bond violators.)

PRISONS 2. Confines convicted state- or federal-level felons, period.

BOTH! 3. Trick question: the Federal Bureau of Prisons sets rules and regulations for both state- and federal-level systems.

BOTH! 4. Another trick questions! The Ohio Department of Rehabilitation and Corrections sets rules and regulations for public, state facilities and jails, in accordance with federal standards.

PRISONS 5. Classifies inmates under 4 levels of security risks: minimum, medium, maximum, supermax/administrative ("problem-children").

70.

JAILS 6. So, **88** county jails (in Ohio) from which you can seek employment!

JAILS 7. The Grand Jury is considered an unbiased but randomly chosen gauge of how society would view the conditions within the jail.

BOTH! 8. **Surprise!** These treatment programs, such as psychological treatment, chemical abuse, anger management, etc…are regularly offered both systems and supported by 12-step fellowships, such as Narcotics and Alcoholics Anonymous.

BOTH! 9. Access to G.E.D./high school equivalency classes is a traditional means of treatment and raises career prospects for the inmates. Logically, however, the jail inmate may not have time to totally complete the program.

PRISONS 10. Time, resources and business-agency partnerships favor prisons.

PROBATION VS. PAROLE

Confused about probation versus parole? Maybe this chart will help:

	PROBATION (Also called Community Supervision Officers)	**PAROLE**
1. GOVERNMENT LEVEL?	*City (misdemeanors) *State (felonies) *Federal (all federal crimes)	*State (felonies) *Federal (all federal crimes)
2. WHEN?	**Before** incarceration	**After** incarceration
3. PRIMARY RESPONSIBILITIES?	*Supervise probationers *Rehabilitation	*Supervise offenders *Control offenders *Reform
4. EDUCATIONAL REQUIREMENT?	**MAY** still be employed with high school at the city-level; bachelor's needed for state and federal.	Bachelor's degree.

MAKING LOCAL OR COUNTY CORRECTIONS YOUR CHOICE

Now you have a general understanding of *what* local corrections entails. **Consider the following points concerning a career in local or county corrections:**

☑ **Job openings:** "There are 118 jail systems in the United States that house over 1000 inmates all of which are located in urban areas" (*Occupational Outlook Handbook, 2002-2003,* n.d., Correctional officers). "About 84,000 people were employed as probation officers and correctional treatment specialists in 2000. Most of these workers work for State or local governments" (*Occupational Outlook Handbook, 2002-2003,* n.d., Probation officers and correctional treatment specialists, Employment.)

☑ **Job outlook:** "Job opportunities for correctional officers are expected to be excellent through 2010. Additional officers (will be) hired to supervise and control a growing inmate population" (*Occupational Outlook Handbook, 2002-2003*, n.d., Correctional officers). "Employment of probation officers and correctional treatment specialists is projected to grow faster than the average for all occupations through 2010" (*Occupational Outlook Handbook, 2002-2003,* n.d., Probation officers and correctional treatment specialists, Job Outlook, paragraph 2).

☑ **Necessary profession:** "Corrections officers maintain order within institutions, enforce rules and regulations, and help ensure that inmates are orderly and obey rules" (*Occupational Outlook Handbook, 2002-2003,* n.d., Correctional officers). Without probation officers, no one would be able to be sentenced to probation!

☑ **Salary:** "Median annual salary for local correctional officers in 2000 nationally was $29,240" (*Occupational Outlook Handbook, 2002-2003,* n.d., Correctional officers, Earnings, paragraph 1). "The middle 50 percent (of probation officers) earned between $30,270 and $49,030" (*Occupational Outlook Handbook, 2002-2003,* n.d., Probation officers and correctional treatment specialists, Earnings).

☑ **High School Education:** "in Ohio, a high school diploma (or equivalent) is required for employment" (*Ohio Department of Rehabilitation and Corrections,* n.d., Education and training requirements). Locally, contact the specific municipal and/or **88** county jails to determine their educational requirements. Remember, if only a high school diploma is required, having "some" college should give you a competitive edge on the written exams and during the oral interview stages of the hiring process.

☑ **Comparison of county-based correctional opportunities:**

	CUYAHOGA CO. SHERIFF'S (Cleveland, Ohio) http://www.cuyahoga.oh.us/sheriff/employees/opportunities.htm	FRANKLIN CO. SHERIFF'S (Columbus, Ohio) http://www.sheriff.franklin.oh.us	MONTGOMERY CO. SHERIFF'S (Dayton, Ohio) http://www.co.montgomery.oh.us/sheriff/Careers/
SALARY	$10.98/hr ($12.59 after 1 year)	$11.95 to $17.22	$29,702 ($33,280 2nd year) +Shift differential
HEALTH INSURANCE	Yes, after 120 days	Yes, medical and prescription drug	Yes, United Health Care
LIFE INSURANCE	$6,000, no cost to the employee	Yes, no details	$50,000 plus option to buy additional
VACATION	1-7 years= 2 weeks 8-14 yrs.= 3 weeks 15-24 yrs.= 4 wks. 25+ yrs.=5 weeks	Yes, no details	1-5 years=2 weeks Up to 5 weeks after 20 years
HOLIDAYS	10 paid	Yes, no details	10 paid & 5 paid personal days
SICK LEAVE	Yes, no details	Yes, no details	Yes, no details
MISCEL-LANEOUS	+Retirement +Credit union +Deferred Compensation	+Retirement +Tuition Reimbursement Program	+Retirement +Vision/Dental +Credit Union +Personal Liability Insurance +Tuition Reimbursement +Deferred Compensation

☑ **CBCF's/Community-based correctional facilities:** are joint efforts between State of Ohio funds and county government. The Director of Operations of a CBCF reports jointly to the local common pleas court and an appointed corrections board. These minimum security facilities house non-violent misdemeanants and lower-level, felony offenders. Offenders attend mandatory educational and employment programs and, upon successful completion of their programs, return to court to have their original sentences reduced (shortened). Unsuccessful offenders may have their original sentence imposed and be transferred to a "regular" correctional institution. So, employment opportunities exist for both correctional officers and program leaders!

☑ **Educational requirements vary for probation officers:** Check with the hiring agency; "but a bachelor's degree in social work, criminal justice, or a related field from a 4-year college or university is usually required" (*Occupational Outlook Handbook, 2002-2003,* n.d., Probation officers and correctional treatment specialists, Training).

☑ **Probation/parole combination**: "In some states (not in Ohio), the job of parole and probation officer is combined" (*Occupational Outlook Handbook, 2002-2003,* n.d., Probation officers and correctional treatment specialists, Nature of Work, paragraph 1). Check the American Probation and Parole Association's website for whether the two positions are combined in any other state.

☑ **Internet links for research:** Simply type in the name of the agency for which you want to work and visit their website. We recommend visiting the Buckeye State Sheriffs' Association or American Probation and Parole Association, listed under "Readings", at the end of this chapter.

☑ **Writing for information:** In a jail setting, write to the American Jail Association; 2052 Day Road, Suite 100; Hagerstown, MD 21740 or The American Probation and Parole Association; P.O. Box 11910; Lexington, KY 40578.

CORRECTIONAL EMPLOYMENT IN OHIO

Public correctional institutions, like their police agency counterparts, are not-for-profit organizations, supported by public monies, such as property taxes, tax levies and bond issues. (Continue reading this chapter if you believe you want to work for public correctional agencies.) Private corrections, on the other hand, is profit-oriented; but, still in the business of corrections. (Read Chapter 7 for additional insights into private correctional opportunities.)

As was stated in Chapter 3 (Looking at Public Law Enforcement), just because you purchased a book on Ohio criminal justice careers, you are not required to limit your search to Ohio. So, let's keep an open mind and start by determining whether you want to work for public corrections in Ohio.

OHIO CORRECTIONS OFFICER-RELATED STATISTICS

First, let's determine which of the following statements apply to *you*:

1. I'd rather be employed within a large correctional institution or system.
2. I'd rather be employed within the smallest correctional institution or system.
3. I'd rather work in direct inmate-supervision or management environments.
4. I'd be more comfortable working within an administrative support unit, which is part of a larger facility or system.
5. I prefer working with inmates who have primarily committed crimes against persons.
6. I'm comfortable working with inmates who have primarily committed property crimes.
7. I'd prefer to work in an environment where the majority of inmates are of the same gender.
8. I'm comfortable working with members of racial minority groups.
9. I'm more at ease working with an educated population (i.e. having at least a high school diploma).
10. I am a female candidate.
11. I am a person of color.
12. I like Ohio.

How did you do? Answers to Ohio Corrections Officer-Related Statistics Quiz:

1 & 2: According to Williams, M. R., King, W. R., & Holcomb, J. E. (2001, p. 23): "Beginning in the early 1980's, Ohio undertook major prison construction initiatives and the number of major (large) institutions eventually increased from seven in 1971 to thirty-one in 2000. And, as of April, 2000, Ohio prisons held more than 46,000 inmates."

3. Per Williams, M. R., King, W. R., & Holcomb, J. E. (2001, p. 26), "Correctional officers supervise inmates within the institutional setting."

4. "The Ohio Department of Rehabilitation also employs those not involved in the direct, daily supervision of inmates…(who) would be the parole officer, the corrections program specialist and the psychological assistant" (Williams, M. R., King, W. R., & Holcomb, J. E., 2001, p. 26).

5. Per Williams, M. R., King, W. R., & Holcomb, J. E. (2001, p. 23): "In 1997, Ohio's prison population mainly held prisoners convicted of crimes against persons, or about 47%."

6. "In 1999, miscellaneous property offenses (17%), and burglary (8%)m accounted in part for new commitments" (Williams, M. R., King, W. R., & Holcomb, J. E. (2001, p. 23).

75.

7.   Per Williams, M. R., King, W. R., & Holcomb, J. E. (2001, p. 23): "Almost 95% of Ohio's prisoners are male." (Note: Ohio Department of Rehabilitation and Corrections-run institutions are segregated by gender.)

8.   Per Williams, M. R., King, W. R., & Holcomb, J. E. (2001, p. 23), and regarding Ohio inmates, "Slightly more than one-half (52%) are Black."

9.   "Almost 85 percent of Ohio's inmates have not graduated from high school or received their General Equivalency Degree" (Williams, M. R., King, W. R., & Holcomb, J. E., 2001, p. 24.

10.   Per Adler, F., Mueller, G. O. W., & Laufer, W. S. (2000, p.**??**), "As of 1997, about 20.6% of corrections officers nationally were female."

11.   Per Adler, F., Mueller, G. O. W., & Laufer, W. S. (2000, p.**??**), "As of 1997, about 32.2% of corrections officers nationally were nonwhite."

12.   Not necessarily a given. But, it should be an easy question to answer!

SEEKING EMPLOYMENT WITH THE OHIO DEPARTMENT OF REHABILITATION AND CORRECTIONS

Facts you'll appreciate if you're seeking employment with ODRC (Ohio Department of Rehabilitation and Corrections, n.d.):

★ **Established system:** The ODRC was created in 1972.

◎ **Responsibilities:** Supervision of adult felons sentenced to at least 6 months in prison and community supervision of inmates released on parole.

 Publicly-operated job opportunities: There are currently 31 **publicly-operated** institutions under ODRC's authority, with over 46,000 inmates

 Privately-operated job opportunities: NorthCoast Correctional Treatment Facility (Grafton) and Lake Erie Correctional Institution (Conneaut) are the State of Ohio's 2 **privately-operated** institutions. (See Chapter 7 for information on these facilities.)

 Variety of positions: at least 90 job descriptions besides corrections officer, which include: Administration, Management Information, Ohio Penal Industries, Education, Training, Industry and Education (T.I.E.), Programming, Fiscal and Research.

★ **3 Institutions for women:** Ohio Reformatory for Women (Marysville), Northeast Pre-Release Center (Cleveland) and Franklin Pre-Release Center (Columbus).

☞ **2 Medical centers, serving both male and female inmates:** Corrections Medical Center (a medical hospital) and Oakwood Correctional Facility (intensive psychiatric treatment facility).

💣 **1 "Supermax" prison:** For inmates requiring administrative (disciplinary) supervision, the Ohio State Penitentiary (Youngstown).

➢ **2 Boot camps:** One for each gender of first-time, non-violent offenders.

☯ **Transfer to other facilities:** As with other state agencies, like the Ohio State Highway Patrol, employees may be subject to transfer to any correctional institution where ODRC deems it necessary.

☯ **Collective bargaining:** Means a seniority system is in place for job assignments at institutional locations.

✴ **Best for last, SALARY:** Median income for state correctional officers in 2000 was $31,860 nationally (*Occupational Outlook Handbook, 2002-2003,* n.d., Correctional officers, Earnings.)

✴ **Great benefits (Department of Administrative Services, n.d., Department of Human Resources, Employee Benefits):**
  ★ **Health, life and disability insurance;**
  ★ **Public Employees Retirement System** where the employee contributes 8.5% of gross wages and employer, 13.31%);
  ★ **Personal leave** of 32 hours per year plus 3 consecutive days for bereavement;
  ★ **Vacation leave** of 80 hours for 1-5 years of service (after working 1 year);
  ★ **Sick leave** accrues at 3.1 hours/80 hours of work;
  ★ **10 Holidays** paid;
  ★ **Optional benefits** of deferred compensation program; credit union; dependent care spending account program; direct deposit of paycheck.

 OTHER STATE OF OHIO CORRECTIONAL OPPORTUNITIES

Under the Ohio Department of Rehabilitation and Corrections (n.d.), there are 4 other corrections-based agencies:

☑ **Bureau of Adult Detention:** "…(P)romotes safe, secure and efficient local jail systems by assisting local officials in their efforts to comply with "Minimum Standards for Jails in Ohio" (*Bureau of adult detention,* n.d.).

☑ **Bureau of Community Sanctions:** "...(D)evelops and improves community corrections programs...(i.e.) halfway houses, community based correctional facilities, and community corrections act programs" (*Bureau of community sanctions,* n.d.).

☑ **Community Corrections, Adult Parole Authority:** "(APA) is responsible for the release and supervision of adult felony inmates returning to local communities from prison, as well as assisting Courts of Common Pleas with sentencing and supervision duties...(operating in) seven regions...(with) approximately 1,150 employees" (*Community corrections, Adult parole authority*).

☑ **Victim Services (1-888-VICTIM4):** "...(B)uilds mutual understanding and open communication among the Department of Rehabilitation and Correction employees, victims, their families, and community service groups" (*Victim services,* n.d.).

A WORD ABOUT FEDERAL CORRECTIONS

A discussion of correctional careers would not be complete without the inclusion of federal-level opportunities. Competition for federal employment is fierce and employment-related issues, unique.

 **FEDERAL CORRECTIONS FACTS**

☹ **Limited job openings:** "About 15,000 (of 457,000) jobs for correctional officers were in Federal correctional institutions" (*Occupational Outlook Handbook, 2002-2003,* n.d., Correctional officers).

☺ **Variety of locations available:** 102 correctional institutions; 6 regional offices (Ohio is in the Northeast Region with 11 male-only facilities, 1 female-only, 4 administrative); 1 Central office/headquarters; 2 training centers; 29 community corrections offices (U.S. Department of Justice, n.d., Federal bureau of prisons).

★ **Job security:** The Federal Bureau of Prisons is currently responsible for 160,000 federal offenders of which about 133,500 are confined to regular corrections and detention centers. The balance are confined to community corrections, juvenile detention and privately-operated prisons. (U.S. Department of Justice, n.d., Federal bureau of prisons).

◎ **Accelerated staffing exists:** If you apply for a job openings at a specifically noted location, the hiring process is accelerated. (See the Federal Bureau of Prisons' website, Employment link.)

☺ **Age limitations:** "Public Law 101-509 establishes a mandatory retirement age of fifty-seven (57) for persons in Federal law enforcement positions" (U.S. Department of Justice, n.d., Federal bureau of prisons). So, you must be appointed by age 37.

☺ **Salary:** "Median annual earnings in the public sector were "37,430 in the Federal Government" (*Occupational Outlook Handbook, 2002-2003,* n.d., Correctional officers, Earnings). "Median annual earnings of probation officers and correctional treatment specialists in 2000 were $38,150" (*Occupational Outlook Handbook, 2002-2003,* n.d., Probation officers and correctional treatment specialists). **Shift differential** exists for night duty and 25% **overtime** pay for working on Sundays (Federal Bureau of Prisons, n.d., Employment benefits).

☑ **Great benefits (Federal Bureau of Prisons, n.d., Employment Benefits):**
   ★ **Commuter subsidy** up to $100 per month;
   ★ **Life insurance** equal to your salary, rounded up to the next thousand dollars;
   ★ **Health insurance** with you paying only 28-40% of the cost;
   ★ **Promotional potential;**
   ★ **Retirement at 50, with 20 years service;**
   ★ **Social Security Plan coverage;**
   ★ **Savings plan;**
   ★ **Vacation** (1-3 years=13 days; 3-15 years=20 days; 15+ years=20 days);
   ★ **Sick leave** of 13 days per year.
   ★ **Transfers** anywhere in the United States, including Hawaii and Puerto Rico.

🗁 **Probation:** Learn more about the United States Probation Offices of Ohio's employment opportunities and requirements--and related court positions. For Akron, Cleveland, Youngstown and Toledo, visit http://www.ohnd.uscourts.gov/ U_S_Probation/u_s_probation.html (website for the United States District Court Northern District of Ohio). For Cincinnati, Columbus and Dayton, visit http://www.ohsp.uscourts.gov for the Ohio Southern Probation Office of the United States District Court.

🗁 **Parole:** Learn more about the United States Parole Commission and useful criminal justice and correctional links by visiting http://www.usdoj.gov/uspc/index.html

☹ **Absence of detailed information:** The *Occupational Outlook Handbook, 2002-2003* (n.d.) does not have a separate heading for parole officers.

CONCLUSION

In this chapter you compared publicly-operated, correctional career opportunities at the local, state and federal levels. You learned the United States Department of Justice's Federal Bureau of Prisons maintains its own regional facilities and manages the federal inmate population. Conversely, while all 50 states maintain their own corrections department, the State of Ohio's Department of Rehabilitation and Corrections not only manages its convicted felons, but also 4 other community corrections-based bureaus. You also discovered there were 2 levels of short-term, detention facilities: municipal jails and those administered by the county sheriff's departments. Also, the inmates of county-level detention facilities do more than serve those sentenced for lesser crimes (usually six months sentences or less): the county facilities really serve anyone awaiting trial or transportation to another government detention facility.

Unfortunately, you may have also been disappointed by the lack of a few pertinent details concerning specific correctional facilities and opportunities. Unless this workbook became as thick as a set of encyclopedias, we could not answer all your questions. Still more disheartening, our career foundation, the *Occupational Outlook Handbook, 2002-2003* (n.d.) was virtually silent on the topic of parole officers and career opportunities. Consequently, we urge you to obtain further information by using Chapter 2's structured interview process. Speak with a veteran corrections practitioner: learn **their** stories and perspectives to help **you** decide your career goals. Visit a local, state or federal correctional facility! Above all, research the specific agency in which you're interested and do **not** give up: there are numerous career opportunities in the corrections field!

SUGGESTED READING

American Correctional Association at http://www.aca.org/

American Jail Association at http://www.corrections.com/aja/index.html

American Probation and Parole Association at http://www.appa-net.org/

Buckeye State Sheriffs' Association at http://www.buckeyesheriffs.org/

The Corrections Connection at http://www.corrections.com/

The Correctional Education Association at http://metalab.unc.edu/icea/

Cuyahoga County Sheriff's Office at http://www.cuyahoga.oh.us/sheriff/employees/opportunities.htm

Franklin County Sheriff's Office at http://www.sheriff.franklin.oh.us/

Montgomery County Sheriff's Office at http://www.co.montgomery.oh.us/sheriff/Careers/

National Institute of Corrections at http://www.nicic.org

Office of the Pardon Attorney at http://www.usdoj.gov/pardon/

United States Department of Justice' Community Relations Service at http://www.usdoj.gov/crs/crs.htm

United States' Corrections Program Office at http://www.ojp.usdoj.gov/cpo/

REFERENCES

Adler, F., Mueller, G. O. W., & Laufer, W. S. (2000). *Criminal justice-An introduction.* Boston, MA: McGraw-Hill.

Cole, G. F. & Smith, C. E. (1999). *Criminal justice in america.* Belmont, CA: Wadsworth/Thomson Learning.

Federal Bureau of Prisons. (n.d.). *Employment benefits.* Retrieved November 12, 2002, from http://www.bop.gov/hrmpg/hrmbenefits.html

Gaines, L. K., Kaune, M., & Miller, R. L. (2001). *Criminal justice in action: the core.* Belmont, CA: Wadsworth/Thomson Learning.

Occupational Outlook Handbook, 2002-2003. (n.d.). *Correctional officers.* Retrieved November 3, 2002, from http://www.bls.gov/oco/ocos156.htm

Occupational Outlook Handbook, 2002-2003. (12-31-01). *News release, 2000-2010 Employment projections.* Retrieved September 1, 2002, from http://www.bls.gov/emp

Occupational Outlook Handbook, 2002-2003. (12-31-01). *News release, table 1. Employment by major industry division, 1990, 2000, and projected 2010.* Retrieved September 1, 2002, from http://www.bls.gov/news.release/Ecopro.t02.htm

Occupational Outlook Handbook, 2002-2003. (12-31-01). *News release, table 2. Employment by major occupational group, 2000, and projected 2010.* Retrieved September 1, 2002, from http://www.bls.gov/news.release/ecopro.t02.htm

Occupational Outlook Handbook, 2002-2003. (n.d.). *Probation officers and correctional treatment specialists.* Retrieved October 21, 2002, from http://www.bls.gov/oco/ocos265.htm

Ohio Department of Rehabilitation and Corrections. (n.d.). *Bureau of adult detention.* Retrieved November 3, 2002, from http://www.drc.state.oh.us/web/BAD.htm

Ohio Department of Rehabilitation and Corrections. (n.d.). *Bureau of community sanctions.* Retrieved November 3, 2002, from http://www.drc.state.oh.us/web/BCS.htm

Ohio Department of Rehabilitation and Corrections. (n.d.). *Community corrections, Adult parole authority.* Retrieved November 3, 2002, from http://www.drc.state.oh.us/web/apa.htm

Ohio Department of Rehabilitation and Corrections. (n.d.). *Victim Services.* Retrieved November 3, 2002, from http://www.drc.state.oh.us/web/VICTIM.htm

Ohio Department of Rehabilitation and Corrections. (n.d.). *Education and training requirements.* Retrieved November 3, 2002, from http://www.drc.state.oh.us/

United States Department of Justice. (n.d.). *Federal bureau of prisons.* Retrieved November 3, 2002, from http://www.bop.gov/

United States Department of Justice. (n.d.). *United states parole commission.* Retrieved November 4, 2002, from http://www.usdoj.gov/uspc/index.html

United States Probation Office. (n.d.). *Northern district of ohio.* Retrieved November 4, 2002, from http://www.ohnd.uscourts.gov/U_S_Probation/u_s_probation.html

United States Probation Office. (n.d). *Southern district of ohio.* Retrieved November 4, 2002, from http://www.ohsp.uscourts.gov/

Williams, M. R., King, W. R., & Holcomb, J. E. (2001). *Criminal justice in ohio.* Needham Heights, MA: Allyn & Bacon.

CHAPTER 7

PRIVATIZATION OF CORRECTIONS

"Stone Walls do not a Prison make, Nor Iron bars a Cage...."
-Richard Lovelace

AFTER READING THIS CHAPTER, YOU SHOULD KNOW
⇨ Why private corrections exists.
⇨ How private corrections are structured.
⇨ How private and public corrections compare.
⇨ The employment outlook in private corrections.
⇨ Positions and titles of those employed in private corrections.
⇨ How to conduct a private-sector job search.

INTRODUCTION

To be succinct, here are the answers to the most frequently asked questions:

1) **Yes, the state could delegate its correctional function to private enterprise.** State governments, frustrated by high repeat offenders (recidivism) rates and ever-increasing prison maintenance costs, looked for an effective alternative (Adler, F., Mueller, G. O. W., & Laufer, W. S., 2000, pp. 352-4).

2) **Yes, private corrections is new to the criminal justice field.** Opened in 1975 (Pennsylvania), one of the first "for profit" prisons was found to be "...better staffed, organized, and equipped than any other program of its size" (Adler, F., Mueller, G. O. W., & Laufer, W. S., 2000, pp. 353).

3) **Yes, private prisons exist throughout the nation.** In 1999, there were 212 private prisons facilities in 32 states, housing 145,000 inmates, with Texas having the most facilities (42), followed by California with 24 (Thomas, n.d., Chart 3).

4) **Yes, Ohio has private corrections.** We have 3 facilities: Lake Erie Correctional Institution (in Ashtabula County); North Coast Correctional Treatment Facility (in Lorain County); Northeast Ohio Correctional Center (a "supermax" in Youngtown).

83.

STRUCTURE OF PRIVATE CORRECTIONAL FACILITIES

This discussion is similar to running a maze: there's only one entrance (privately-run, correctional facilities), but there may be more than one exit. Confused? Don't be. **There are really only two operational styles:**

◎ **Collaboration:** Here, the private corporation collaborates with a unit of government, such as the county-level (jail) or state-level (prison). For example, the North Coast Correctional Treatment Facility (Grafton) is built by the Ohio Department of Rehabilitation and Corrections (ODRC); but, operated by CiviGenics Corporation. Inmates have either been convicted of a felony or have documented history of drug and alcohol abuse. Their mission and philosophy emphasize treatment and recidivism reduction (ODRC, 2000, Mission).

◎ **Subcontract basis:** For example, management of a portion of Tennessee's correctional facilities were turned over to CCA/Corrections Corporation of America for a contracted price (Adler, F., Mueller, G. O. W., & Laufer, W. S., 2000, p. 353).

PRIVATE VS. PUBLIC CORRECTIONS

So, which is more effective, private or public corrections? You decide for yourself.

SUPPORTERS OF PRIVATE CORRECTIONS

Supporters of private corrections cite the following statistics:

★ **Opportunities for inmates:** Idleness was reduced while inmates had opportunities to earn wages and receive vocational training, both of which can be used post-release (Adler, F., Mueller, G. O. W., & Laufer, W. S., 2000, p. 354).

★ **Opportunities for employment:** Options are endless, the employee can work with male or female inmates; adult or juvenile offenders; minimum, medium, or maximum-security levels; jails versus prison; pre-release facilities and, at least in the case of Corrections Corporation of America, Immigration and Naturalization Service-related facilities (Corrections Corporation of America, n.d. Career Seeker).

★ **Reduced escape ratio:** "CCA prisons' escape ratio was less than one-third the national average, based on the most recent data available (1999-2000). This places CCA among the best performing systems in the country" (Corrections Corporation of America, n.d., CCA Company Overview).

★ **Improved recidivism rates:** "According to a recent University of Florida study and report to the Florida State Legislature, inmates in privately managed prisons were 27% less likely to become repeat offenders" (Corrections Corporation of America, n.d., Corrections Overview).

★ **Reduction of overcrowded conditions:** "Available beds in private correctional facilities help reduce overcrowded conditions and thus improve the overall operations in publicly operated prison and jail systems" (Corrections Corporation of America, n.d., Corrections Overview).

★ **Employee benefits:** CCA (n.d., Career Seeker) state benefits for their employees include: training; promotional opportunities; insurance (health, dental, vision, life, accidental death/dismemberment); personal leave; short-term disability; sick leave; 10 paid holidays and a 401(k) pension plan.

 CONCERNS ABOUT PRIVATE CORRECTIONS

Non-supporters of private corrections have the following issues:

💣 **What standards ultimately govern the operation of private facilities?** Who has jurisdiction, especially if there are conflicted concerns, Federal Bureau of Prisons or the pertinent state government?

💣 **Who will monitor, inspect and sanction (discipline) the operations?** For example, in the case of the sudden death of an inmate, who investigates? Who investigates a "walk away" or an "escape"?

💣 **Does the private corporate entity have sufficient financial resources to offer continuing services?** In the search of profit, does the quantity and quality of programs and services suffer? How would we know?

85.

💣 **If private corporations are non-union, are the employees being treated well?** What recourses do employees have, only the corporation's grievance procedure? Is the corporation's profit being made at the expense of the employee's paycheck?

💣 **Can we even keep track of the players?** For example, Prison Realty dissolved its old partnership to merge with CCA (*PR Newswire*, 2000, June 30). Wackenhut Corporation is now part of Group 4 Falck (Copenhagen) and the Group 4 Falck homepage asks whether you'd rather see their website in the Danish language.

WHAT IS THE EMPLOYMENT OUTLOOK?

☑ **Clear trend toward contracting for correctional services** (Adler, F., Mueller, G. O. W., & Laufer, W. S., 2000, p. 354).

☺ **Business is booming:** Corrections Corporation of America, now part of the Prison Realty Trust, "…has approximately 60,000 beds and currently houses approximately 53,000 inmates in 61 facilities…21 states (plus 29 municipalities) and the District of Columbia (Corrections Corporation of American, n.d., Company Overview).

◎ **Industry leaders:** CCA and Prison Realty alone, account for approximately 69,000 beds, in 77 facilities, including District of Columbia, United Kingdom, Puerto Rico and Australia (*PR Newswire,* n.d., 6-30-00). Another industry leader, Wackenhut Corporation, now offers prison and inmate management services, has over 40,000 employees and headquarters in Palm Beach, Florida (Wackenhut, n.d., homepage).

🏳 **Employment opportunities:** Private corrections is not limited to correctional officers and institutional management and services. These private corporations also address correctional design, construction, renovation of jails or prisons, in addition to performing short- and long-distance inmate transportation services.

☎ **Call about juvenile facilities.** Private corporations aren't limited to adult offenders; so, why should you be? Check companies such as Children's Comprehensive and Res-Care concerning privately-run facilities for housing and managing juvenile offenders with behavioral and delinquency problems, developmental disabilities, mental illness and chemical abuse issues (The Motely Fools' Evening News, 1997, February, 21).

- ☯ **Employee qualifications:** Will be addressed in the next chapter. However, it's sufficient to note that applicants for private prison employment are expected to meet the same industry standards as those employed in public correctional facilities. Criteria would include, but not be limited to, passing certain physical standards; basic knowledge tests; psychological screening; polygraph testing; oral interviews; background and medical checks.

- 💣 **Employee earnings:** The Ohio Department of Rehabilitation and Corrections currently pays $12.00 per hour for a corrections officer (ODRC, n.d., Handbook). To attract qualified employees, private corporations would have to remain competitive regarding employee salaries. However, private corporations are profit-oriented; consequently, prospective employees may be facing a slightly lower pay rate. For further details, contact the prospective employer of your choice.

POSITIONS & TITLES IN PRIVATE CORRECTIONS

Private prison operations mirror those of the public sector correctional institutions. Position availability, work environment, earnings, benefits and promotional opportunities vary greatly within each category. However, you can improve the likelihood of being employment and achieving workplace success by having criminal justice experience or education, dual language proficiency or the professional license or business certification appropriate for your chosen position. Be sure any such professional assets are highlighted in your job application and resume. (See Chapter 12 for job applications and resumes!)

Do any of these positions sound interesting to you?

☑ **ADMINISTRATIVE OR OPERATIONAL DUTIES:**

- ✷ **Warden:** Starting at the top, the warden has the overall, superintendent-style control over the correctional facility.

- ✷ **Business Officer (or Manager):** Anyone who deals with institutional employees and labor-management issues.

- ✷ **Case Manager:** correctional practitioners charged with documenting the overall care and correction of individual inmates, usually from initial admission, to transfer to a home institution, to eventual discharge to post-release control.

* **Institutional Identification Officer:** Responsible for required photographing, finger-printing and related tasks, the I.I.O. "processes" the inmate's initial admission to the correctional facility.

* **Training Officer:** Anyone who **only** provides tactical (in-service) training and instruction to **employees**, concerning a variety of operational and procedural topics.

☑ **PROGRAMMING & SUPPORT FOR INMATES:**

▭ **T.I.E. Officer (or Deputy):** Officers involved in <u>t</u>raining, <u>i</u>ndustrial and <u>e</u>ducational programs for **inmates**.

▭ **Teacher and Teaching Supervisor:** Licensed educators responsible for educational instruction within prison programs. Upon entry to the institution, the inmates are classified according to current educational level. Then, the teachers provide classification-based instruction, both in a general classroom and individually, one-on-one, with a specific inmate.

▭ **Guidance Counselor:** Aligned with the educational staff, the counselor assists the inmate in career and advanced educational opportunities, especially upon discharge, back into the community.

▭ **Substance Abuse Program Coordinator:** Those practitioners charged with conducting individual and group sessions for the benefit of inmates having substance abuse or substance dependency problems. Usually certified in chemical dependency counseling, they may also work closely with 12-step, fellowship programs, such as the Institutional Programming personnel of Narcotics Anonymous.

☑ **MEDICAL PROFESSIONALS:**

☞ **Psychological Assistant:** A person who assists the licensed, mental health official in administering and assessing mental health conditions of inmates, through standardized testing and in-person interviewing sessions.

☞ **Nurse:** Licensed medical practitioner who provides in-house medical care under the direct supervision of doctors employed by the correctional departmental or facility.

☑ **SPECIALISTS:**

◎ **Penal Industries Manager:** A professional with a special occupational or vocational background, who works for the Penal Industries Division of the Ohio Department of Rehabilitation and Corrections. The manager supervises inmates involved in the product or service to the institution, itself, or any outside customers. For example, if the inmates upgrade computers for sale at a minimal cost to educational institutions, the manager would oversee the inmates performing the upgraded, sale and dissemination of the computers.

THE PRIVATE-SECTOR JOB SEARCH

In the next chapter, the specifics concerning career testing and training in public sector-based corrections will be addressed. If you are interested in private-sector corrections, however, still read the next chapter: there are strong parallels between private- and public-sector pre-employment screening, just as there are for positions and titles.

Meanwhile, consider the following suggestions to improve your employability:

📁 **Update your resume:** Use the formal application process for private prison corporations.

💣 **Do not email your resume, unless specifically noted on the position posting:** we're a traditional career field and email is not "traditional"--it's even considered rude to contact a criminal justice professional for the first time via email. If you want respect, follow the rules of the field: mail or drop-off the resume!

◎ **Target ALL prospective employers in your area:** Note the employers in your area. Check criminal justice career days at the local college or university.

☑ **Check the reputation of ALL prospective employers:** Read the newspaper, listen to the news, check their website, contact the Better Business Bureau.

🏳 **Flag a "short-list" of potential employers:** If possible, ask for a tour of the private facility, talk with the employee-tour guide, solicit his or her input.

✂ **Cut the list of potential employers to preferred employers:** Apply for the position and keep updated as to the professionalism of the employer. Physical and operational structure of the facility, labor-management relations or inmate-programming, health and safety can all change. Keep listening to the media, visiting the employer's website and checking the financial status of the corporation.

CONCLUSION

You've just experienced a "snapshot" of the still-developing private correctional industry. In particular, you learned concerns over budget, overcrowding, recidivism and escapes made the private prison alternative attractive to state and federal governments. Therefore, private-sector brick-and-mortar correctional facilities arose and mirrored their public-sector counterparts, despite political and philosophical opposition. Consequently, private-sector employment opportunities now mirror those of public-sector facilities.

Yet, differences between public- and private-sector employment do exist. The financial philosophy of "corrections-for-profit" alters the labor-management relationship and forces you to more closely investigate prospective employers. Consequently, you were urged to investigate the historical and organization structure of the employing corporation and continue to update employer-related information **before** making any decision about your choice of careers or employers. Despite some professional growing pains, the evidence is clear: the private prison industry is here to stay and, most likely, will expand. Why don't you take advantage of the growing industry and career opportunities?

SUGGESTED READING

American Correctional Association (especially for its career development link and on-line corrections academy) at http://www.aca.org

Corrections Corporation of America at http://www.correctionscorp.com

Group 4 Falck (correctional corporation) at http://www.group4falck.com

Lake Erie Correctional Institution at http://www.drc.state.oh.us/Public/laeci.htm

NorthCoast Correctional Treatment Facility at http://www.drc.state.oh.us/public/ncctf.htm

Northeast Ohio Correctional Center (Corrections Corporation of America's Supermax facility at Youngstown, Ohio) at http://www.correctionscorp.com/act_bystate. cfm?f_success=facilities&state=Ohio

Wackenhut Corporation at http://www.wackenhut.com

REFERENCES

Adler, F., Mueller, G. O. W., & Laufer, W. S. (2000). *Criminal justice: An introduction.* Boston, MA: McGraw-Hill.

Corrections Corporation of America. (n.d.). *Career Seeker.* Retrieved November 7, 2002, from http://www.correctionscorp.com/main/career.html

Corrections Corporation of America. (n.d.). *CCA company overview.* Retrieved November 7, 2002, from http://www.correctionscorp.com/overview/company overview.html

Corrections Corporation of America. (n.d.). *Corrections overview.* Retrieved November 7, 2002, from http://www.correctionscorp.com/overview/ corrections overview.html

Group 4 Falck. (n.d.). *Group 4 Falck, Global solutions.* Retrieved November 7, 2002, From http://www.group4falck.com/object.php?obj=4d000c

Ohio Department of Rehabilitations and Corrections & CiviGenics Corporation. (2000). *Program Informational Handbook.* Grafton, OH: North Coast Correctional Treatment Facility

PR Newswire. (2000, June 30). *Prison reality and pacific life terminate agreement: Prison realty to merge with corrections corporation of america.* Retrieved November 7, 2002, from http://findarticles.com

The Motely Fools' Evening News. (1997, February 21). Retrieved from http://www. Fool.com/Decathlon.1997/SubscriberOnLine970627B.htm

Thomas, Charles. (1999). *Number of private prison facilities by geographical location, united states.* Retrieved October 2, 2002, from http://www.crim.ufl.edu/pcp/ census/1999/Chart3.html

Wackenhut Corporation. (n.d.). *Homepage.* Retrieved November 7, 2002, from http:// www.wackenhut.com/about/index.html (or, through a link from Group 4 Falck's homepage).

CHAPTER 8

LOOKING AT CORRECTIONS TESTING

"Let me tell you the secret that has led me to my goal.
My strength lies solely in my tenacity."
-Louis Pasteur

AFTER READING THIS CHAPTER, YOU SHOULD KNOW
⇨ Elimination factors for corrections.
⇨ How to find corrections testing-related FAQ's/Frequently Asked Questions.
⇨ The standard testing procedures for county-level corrections.
⇨ What the State of Ohio employment process includes.
⇨ What the Ohio Corrections Assessment process entails.
⇨ What Ohio training is required after employment.
⇨ The testing procedures for federal-level corrections.

INTRODUCTION

You just investigated your occupational preferences for public corrections in Chapter 6 and analyzed the wide spectrum of employment and promotional opportunities for private corrections in Chapter 7. But, *how* do you attain that coveted public-sector corrections position, and what can exclude you from applying? What testing procedures are involved in the hiring or assessment center process? Lastly, *why* does this paragraph sound so similar to its law enforcement mirror image in Chapter 5?

Let's start this chapter by clarifying that last issue. Both law enforcement and corrections are executive branches of federalism. Therefore, there will be similarities in philosophies, goals and *general* pre-employment screening procedures. However, the *specific* hiring processes and qualifications will be *specific* to either corrections or law enforcement.

Thus, testing procedures can now be examined through a comparison of local-, state- and federal-level corrections positions. Again, we don't want to deny you any career opportunity. So, we've included information concerning the Federal Bureau of Prisons. While special care will be given to detailed information on testing stages, you should refer to the suggested readings for any additional questions you may have. For details on municipal corrections, we urge you to directly contact the municipality of your choice.

ELIMINATION FACTORS FOR CORRECTIONS

Do these county-level, corrections-based "skeletons" exist in your closet?

CORRECTIONS AGENCY	FACTORS WHICH MAY ELIMINATE AN APPLICANT	SUGGESTION: VISIT THEIR WEBSITE
1. **CUYAHOGA CO. SHERIFF'S OFFICE**	-Pending criminal charges. -Convicted, non-traffic misdemeanor in past 5 years, anywhere in U.S. -Felony conviction, past 10 years, anywhere in U.S. -Driver's license suspended or revoked, past 5 years, in U.S. -Habitually used intoxicating beverages or narcotics, past 10 years.	http://www.cuyah oga.oh.us/sheriff/ *From their application form
2. **HAMILTON CO. SHERIFF'S OFFICE**	-Not meet entry-level requirements. -Fail any step in pre-employment process. -No further details given.	http://www.sheriff .franklin.oh.us/offi ce/selection.asp
3. **MONTGOMERY CO. SHERIFF'S OFFICE**	-Felony conviction. -Misdemeanor conviction within last 5 years or 2 or more misdemeanors at any time. -Conviction of drug possession or sales (excluding marijuana) -Convicted of sex offense, bodily harm. -Convicted re gun control ordinance. -Serious traffic, 2 DUS or 6+ points. -Serious employment-re conduct within last 5 years -Failure to obey court decisions. -Other than honorable discharge. -Bribery, false statements/alarms. -Member of criminal/violent group. -Pattern of alcohol, drug abuse or gambling.	http://www.co.mo ntgomery.oh.us/sh eriff/Careers/disqu alifying.html **NOTE: To provide a more succinct answer, we only listed the key disqualifying _categories_. For additional details on any category, refer to the website.**

Could these factors eliminate you from Ohio or federal-based corrections?

CORRECTIONS AGENCY	FACTORS WHICH MAY ELIMINATE AN APPLICANT	SUGGESTION: VISIT THEIR WEBSITE
1. **ODRC-ADULT PAROLE AUTHORITY**	-Per website, not meet entry-level requirements. No further details. -- -Per telephone conversation, add: No DUI convictions.	http://www.drc.state.oh.us ----------------------- R. Sibiliski (personal communication, November 13, 2002).
2. **UNITED STATES DEPARTMENT OF JUSTICE'S FEDERAL BUREAU OF PRISONS**	-Criminal record. -Maybe past drug behavior: "(t)he Department of Justice has a zero tolerance for illegal drug usage." -Maybe family member in prison. -Derogatory credit history. -- -Felony conviction. -Domestic violence conviction.	http://www.bop.gov/hrmpg/hrmfaa.html -------------------- https://jobs.qfuickhire.com/scripts/bop.exe/runuserinfo

CORRECTIONS TESTING-RELATED FAQ'S

Anticipating your 3 unanswered questions, we've provided the following answers:

1. **True, there really isn't much information on municipal-level corrections.** There are too many local jails to explore and, besides, the book isn't that long.

2. **No, we didn't include polygraph testing procedures in this chapter.** Since we tested your knowledge and gave you great information under Chapter 3, we didn't want to be redundant nor boring.

3. **No, there isn't much information on written examinations.** We heard, "It's job-related" and "fair to both college- and non-college educated applicants" so often, we gave up trying to get any more details.

"STANDARD" TESTING AT THE COUNTY-LEVEL

Continue reading for detail on 3 examples of county-level correctional testing:

	CUYAHOGA CO. SHERIFF'S (Cleveland, Ohio) http://www.cuyahoga.oh.us/sheriff/employees/opportunities.htm	FRANKLIN CO. SHERIFF'S (Columbus, Ohio) http://www.sheriff.franklinl.oh.us/	MONTGOMERY CO. SHERIFF'S (Dayton, Ohio) http://www.co.montgomery.oh.us/sheriff/Careers/
1. MINIMUM AGE?	21 years old.	18 years old.	18 years old.
2. EDUCATION?	High school or GED.	High school or GED; *"prefer bachelor's, associate's in law enforcement, or military or civilian corrections experience."*	High school or GED.
3. WRITTEN EXAM?	Unknown.	Yes, no further details.	Yes & keyboard at 30+ words per minute
4. PSYCHOLOGICAL EXAM?	Unknown.	Yes, after conditional offer of employment.	Yes, no further details.
5. BACKGROUND CHECK?	Yes. (See disqualifying factors.)	Yes.	Yes.
6. ORAL INTERVIEW?	Unknown.	Yes.	Yes.
7. PHYSICAL AGILITY?	Unknown.	Unknown.	Unknown.
8. POLYGRAPH?	Unknown.	Yes.	Yes.
9. MEDICAL EXAMS?	Drug and alcohol testing.	After conditional employment offer.	Drug and pre-employment.

(For specific information regarding responsibilities and job descriptions, visit the pertinent website. For information regarding salary and benefits, re-visit Chapter 6.)

STARTING THE STATE EMPLOYMENT PROCESS

Why start working for the State of Ohio? Because "(t)he Department of Rehabilitation and Correction is Ohio's largest state agency, with over 15,000 employees. About half of those employees are corrections officers" (Ohio Department of Rehabilitation and Correction, n.d., FAQ)

 THE STATE OF OHIO CIVIL SERVICE APPLICATION

You can apply for either a corrections or parole officer's position in the traditional manner: pick up a hard-copy State of Ohio Civil Service Application (Form GEN 4268). These forms can be obtained at any Department of Administrative Services' Department of Human Resource office i.e. the Ohio Bureau of Employment Services or a "One-Stop Employment and Training Centers" (Ohio Department of Administrative Services, n.d., Department of human resources: instructions for job applicants).

Furthermore, Ohio now lets you apply on-line, presuming the hiring agency is itself on-line. To apply, complete a job search, read about civil service examinations and/or obtain additional testing services information, visit the Ohio Department of Administrative Services, Human Resources Department's Instructions for Job Applicants at http://www.state.oh.us/das/dhr/applinfo.html

 GENERAL STATE OF OHIO CIVIL SERVICE PROCESS

According to the Ohio Department of Administrative Services (n.d., Instructions for Job Applicants), the general State of Ohio Civil Service Employment Processing includes:

☑ Completion of State of Ohio Civil Service Application;
☑ Meet minimum and position-specific qualifications;

☑ Pass Civil Service test (55 state position require a passing score);

☑ Pass structured interview (each applicant responds to same set of questions);

☑ Pass any other test as decided by the state agency.

 OHIO CORRECTIONS ASSESSMENT PROCESS

According to the Ohio Department of Rehabilitation and Corrections (n.d., Ohio Corrections Assessment Center), to be hired by ODRC you must:

🖎 **Completion of State of Ohio Civil Service Application.** (Sorry, we couldn't resist checking to see if you were reading or just skimming: there's a lot of information here and it makes more sense if you're awake.)

🖎 **Successfully pass Correction Officer Assessment**, if applying for either a corrections officer or parole officer position.

	CORRECTIONS OFFICER	**PAROLE OFFICER**
1. CORRECTION OFFICER VIDEO TEST?	Yes. No further details.	No.
2. PHYSICAL AGILITY TEST?	Yes: ¾ mile run; lifting & moving 50 pound locker; search and shakedown of bunk.	No.
3. AMES/ADULT MEASUREMENT OF ESSENTIAL SKILL?	Yes. No further details.	No.
4. INTERVIEW?	Yes. No further details.	Yes. No further details.
5. BACKGROUND INVESTIGATION?	Yes, including FBI/BCI fingerprinting. (See Chapter 3 re BCI/Ohio's Bureau of Criminal Identification & Investigation.)	Yes, FBI/BCI finger-printing.
6. DRUG TEST?	Yes. No further details.	Yes. No further details.
7. PROBATIONARY PERIOD?	365 days.	365 days.

TRAINING REQUIRED AFTER EMPLOYMENT

Again, according to the Ohio Department of Rehabilitation and Corrections (n.d., Ohio Corrections Assessment Center), after being hired by ODRC you must complete the following required training:

	CORRECTIONS OFFICER	PAROLE OFFICER
1. CORRECTIONS TRAINING ACADEMY? (IN ORIENT)	Yes, 5 weeks of training (4 of which are consecutive).	Yes, 3 consecutive weeks.
2. CERTIFIED IN UNARMED SELF-DEFENSE?	Yes and re-certify every year. (No "within 1 year of hiring" statement made.)	Yes, **within one year from date of hire!**
3. QUALIFY WITH FACILITY WEAPONS?	Yes and re-qualify every year.	No, but "…may be required to carry and maintain proficiency in firearm and/or pepper spray."
4. UNUSUAL WORKING CONDITIONS?	Surprisingly, no details given.	-Requires travel. -May be in high crime areas or institutional setting. -Risk of violence & vicious animals. -Risk of communicable diseases. -Unpleasant working conditions. -Unpleasant environmental hazards. -Must provide own transportation. -On 24-hour call. -Monitors, collects & transports urine samples for testing. -May carry firearms. -May use pepper spray.*

*No, honest, this is *not* a typographical error. The ODRC cited these conditions under Parole Officer, *not* Corrections Officer!

FEDERAL-LEVEL CORRECTIONS TESTING

According to USAJOBS Jobs Result List (n.d., Bureau of Prisons), the following pre-employment screening for the Federal Bureau of Prisons entails:

☑ **Meeting KSA's** (Knowledge, Skills and Abilities, sound familiar? We just used the Ohio term of SKA's in our references.)

☑ **Take advantage of Veteran's preferential hiring:** 5 point preference to veterans and 10 points for disabled veterans. (See their website for details.)

☑ **Pass the Physical Abilities Test (at Glynco, GA):** "Walking/standing up to an hour; seeing a human figure at a distance of one quarter mile or a target at 250 yards; hearing and detecting movement; using firearms; performing self-defense movements; running an extended distance; climbing stairs; lifting, dragging, and carrying objects; and smelling smoke and drugs" (U.S. Department of Justice, n.d., BOP-FAQ, Employment and online applications).

☑ **Pass re-employment medical examination.** (No further details.)

☑ **Pass drug screening** (and be willing to be subjected to random drug testing.)

☑ **Pass background security investigation.**

CONCLUSION

Since you just completed this chapter, go take a break, you deserve it!. There really isn't any other way to do the content for a chapter like this, other than use lists and charts. But, it is more demanding for you to digest information contained in such a format. Besides, you probably re-visited our polygraph quiz in Chapter 5 and, again, aced it!

By now, you know why we didn't include municipal corrections in this chapter. You also discovered that while there are more details on elimination factors at the county- than the state- and federal-levels, having "skeletons in your closet" can disqualify you from any level, corrections positions. To prevent your being disqualified for employment during the pre-employment process, you now know what testing procedures are required at the each corrections level…and whether you could pass them.

Again, you were probably as disappointed as we were by the limited information on probation. But. remind yourself that the corrections field has unique concerns which do not effect our police brethren. Corrections must be careful about disseminating or posting information where offenders and offender's families can readily find and use the information against correctional employees and facilities. So, no, the corrections field is neither backward nor slow: just a private and protective employer.

SUGGESTED READING

American Correctional Association at http://www.aca.org/

American Jail Association at http://www.corrections.com/aja/index.html

American Probation and Parole Association at http://www.appa-net.org/

Buckeye Sheriffs' Association for Ohio counties not analyzed in this chapter, visit http://www.buckeyesheriffs.org/

Ohio Department of Rehabilitation and Corrections' Corrections Training Academy at http://www.drc.state.oh.us/web/cta.htm

REFERENCES

Cuyahoga County Sheriff's Office. (n.d.). *Employment opportunities.* Retrieved November 12, 2002, from http://www.cuyahoga.oh.us/sheriff/employees/opportunities.htm

Franklin County Sheriff's Office. (n.d.). *Employment opportunities.* Retrieved November 12, 2002, from http://www.sheriff.franklin.oh.us/office/selection.asp

Montgomery County Sheriff's Office. (n.d.). *Careers.* Retrieved November 12, 2002, from http://www.co.montgomery.oh.us/sheriff/Careers/

Ohio Department of Rehabilitation and Corrections. (n.d.). *FAQs/Frequently asked questions.* Retrieved November 11, 2002, from http://www.drc.state.oh.us/web/FAQ.htm

Ohio Department of Administrative Services. (n.d.). *Department of human resources: Instructions for job applicants.* Retrieved November 12, 2002, from http://www.drc.state.oh.us/das/dhr/das/dhr/applinfo.html

Ohio Department of Rehabilitation and Corrections. (1999, April 1). *Announcement for Corrections Officer #36531: Assessment Center.*

Ohio Department of Rehabilitation and Corrections. (n.d.) *Homepage.* Retrieved November 11, 2002, from http://www.drc.state.oh.us

Sibiliski, R. (2002, November 13). *Personal communication:* Training & assessment officer, ODRC/Adult Parole Authority, Elyria, Ohio APA District Office.

United States Department of Justice. (n.d.). *Federal bureau of prisons: FAQ's.* Retrieved November 13, 2002 from http://www.bop.gov/hrmpg/hrmfaq.html

United States Department of Justice. (n.d.). *Federal bureau of prisons: BOP-Hires.* Retrieved November 13, 2002 from http://www.bop.gov/hrmpg/hrmfaq.html

CHAPTER 9

PRIOR PLANNING PREVENTS POOR POSITIONS

"...(T)he three rules of success are prepare, prepare, prepare."
-Duane Brown & Linda Brooks

AFTER READING THIS CHAPTER, YOU SHOULD KNOW
⇨ How to define a realistic plan.
⇨ *What* you are seeking, a job or a career.
⇨ *Who* will be involved in your plan.
⇨ *Where* you should seek employment.
⇨ *When* you should seek employment.
⇨ *How much* money is involved in seeking employment.
⇨ *How* do you set your employment goal.
⇨ What are your occupational goals.

INTRODUCTION

"A plan is an anticipated series of activities or path that leads to a goal" (Brown & Brooks, 1991, p. 246). A *realistic* plan should be *appropriate* (built on an honest and accurate assessment of your skills, knowledge, abilities and values), *affordable* (address how you will pay for this goal) and, especially, *attainable* (likely to be completed in a timely manner). For example, obtaining a bachelor's degree is a realistic goal for state-level, criminal justice employment. Consequently, a *realistic* plan should address your ability to balance family and work obligations; pay the bills (food, housing, clothing, transportation, tuition and books); maintain your sanity, within a time frame of your choosing. If the plan does not accomplish these tasks, it is neither realistic nor a plan.

In this chapter, *you* will formulate your own realistic plan, using the proven method of answering the basic questions of any systematic research: what, who, where, when, how much, why (when the reason is *not* self-evident) and how? Then, through self-assessment, *you* will determine *your realistic,* occupational goal.

WHAT ARE YOU SEEKING: A JOB OR CAREER?

Are YOU looking for a Job or Career?

	JOB	CAREER
1. LONGEVITY?	"I'll stay as long as I want to. They have no hold on me."	**TRUE OR FALSE:** "I plan on staying for at least 2-3 years."
2. LOYALTY?	"They pay me, I'll be loyal."	**TRUE OR FALSE:** "I believe in being a team player".
3. SHARED GOALS?	"If I wanted to know my co-workers, I'd invite them to my house."	**TRUE OR FALSE:** "If we know each other, we'll work together better."
4. SHARED SKILLS & KNOWLEDGE?	"Why should I teach some-one else my job? They may do it better than I do"	**TRUE OR FALSE:** "There's no 'I' in 'team'!"
5. RECOGNITION AND/OR ADVANCE-MENT?	"The only promotion I want is a raise in pay."	**TRUE OR FALSE:** "I want to eventually be promoted up the chain of command."
6. EDUCATIONAL OUTLOOK?	"Unless I get a financial incentive, I'm not completing any classes."	**TRUE OR FALSE:** "Even if I don't get re-imbursed, I want to keep on learning for *me*.
7. PROFESSIONAL OUTLOOK?	"If they're not one of us, you can't trust them."	**TRUE OR FALSE:** "I believe I can make a difference in my community."
8. SUMMARIZATION?	"Clock in & clock out."	**TRUE OR FALSE:** "I can't imagine working at anything else."

SELF-ASSESSMENT: The more "TRUE" answers you had, the more likely you're looking for a career.

WHO IS INVOLVED IN THE PLAN?

The key personnel in this plan are YOU and your INSIDERS (people whose opinions are important to you). Let's start with the basics, YOU.

 YOU: YOUR PROFESSIONAL SELF-ASSESSMENT

Summarize your findings from Chapter 1 to answer these questions:
1.   **My top 5 effective skills are:**

_____   _____

_____   _____

_____

2.   **The 5 abilities I value the most are:**

_____   _____

_____   _____

_____

3.   **My personality is more:**
         ☑ Introverted (reserved)   OR   Extroverted (outgoing)
         ☑ Logical (orderly)   OR   "Wing-it person" (intuitive)
         ☑ "People-person"   OR   "Idea-person"
         ☑ Team-player   OR   Leader

4.   I am more **LEFT-brained** OR ![skull] **RIGHT-brained**.

5.   **My 5 most important, personal core values are:**

A. _____

B. _____

C. _____

D. _____

E. _____

 **YOUR INSIDERS**

The 10 key people in my life (family and friends) who are important to me:

NAMES	SUPPORT MY CAREER CHOICE? (DETAILS?)	UNSUPPORTIVE? (DETAILS?)
1.		
2.		
3.		
4.		
5.		
6.		
7.		
8.		
9.		
10.		

SELF-ASSESSMENT:
☺ Do you have more supportive than unsupportive insiders in your life?
☺ Can you pursue your occupational goal, knowing there are unsupportive insiders?
💣 Are you pursuing this occupation because YOU want to or someone else wants it?
💣 Do you need to change your occupational dream?

WHERE SHOULD YOU SEEK EMPLOYMENT?

Summarize your findings from Chapter 2, to answer the following questions:

1. Visualize and describe your "dream" occupation. _____

    _____

2. In no particular order, name the top 5 things you want from an employer?

    _____   _____

    _____   _____

    _____

3. I would prefer to work for an employer who is:
    - ☑ Traditional   OR   Community-oriented
    - ☑ Larger (35+ employees)   OR   Smaller
    - ☑ Specialists   OR   Generalists
    - ☑ Private Industry   OR   Public Industry
    - ☑ Local/grass roots   OR   State- or Federally-funded

SELF-ASSESSMENT: My top 5 occupational choices at this point are:

WHERE EMPLOYED?	HOW CAN I FIND OUT IF THEY'RE HIRING?	HAVE I CHECKED IF THEY'RE HIRING?
1.		
2.		
3.		
4.		
5.		

WHEN SHOULD YOU SEEK EMPLOYMENT?

Consider whether this is a good PERSONAL time for you to seek employment:

💣 Do I want to change employment.
☑ I want to meet new people.
☑ I am interested in changing your current lifestyle.
☑ My physical fitness level appropriate for hiring standards.
☑ My sense of self and psychological well-being are strong.
💣 I have no criminal record which needs explaining.
💣 I have no criminal record in the process of being expunged.
♫ I do not have a driving history which needs explaining.
☎ Call the credit bureau: I have an A-01 credit rating.
☯ I have no major stressors in my life. *(Really? Just not fooling yourself? Read on.)*
☯ I am not getting married or divorced.
☯ I am not having a relative or baby move into my life.
☯ I am not in the process of buying a house or condominium.
☯ I am not in the process of moving to a new residence.
☞ I have a reliable car.
☞ I do not have an extremely sick relative.
☞ I do not have an extremely sick friend.
☞ I am not attending college.

Consider whether this is a good PROFESSIONAL time for you to seek employment:

1. **Observational Finances?** (*WHY?* "Last hired, first fired.")
    ☑ Media review? Allegations or hints of scandals and/or mismanagement?
    ☑ Position postings in newspaper or on website?
    ☑ Building is neat, clean and in good repair?
    ☑ Equipment (vehicles, uniforms, gear) are neat, clean and in good repair?

2. **Organization?** (*WHY?* Re-organization is usually a warning flag**.**)
    ☹ Consolidation of departments, dispatch, and/or services to save money?
    ☺ Corrections: charging for incarceration? Accepting other agency's inmates?
    ☺ Beginning of fiscal year. (More likely to afford you.)

3. **State- & Federal-support available?** (*WHY?* More governmental support, more solvency and stability.) Again, check the media for clues.

4.   **Age of personnel?** [*WHY?* If only rookies (under 5 years) and almost retirees (15+ years), then mid-level personnel have left. Why? Were they tired of outdated equipment, limited specialized training, low/absent raises, unfunded promotions?]

5.   **Unionized climate?** (*WHY?* If union, do they have better salary and benefits or friction over labor issues? If non-union, better salary and benefits as incentives *not* to organize or too afraid to organize?)

SELF-ASSESSMENT: is it the right time to seek employment? YES/NO
💣* If it isn't the right time to seek employment, what actions do you have to take now?

_____

_____

☯ When *would* you be ready to seek employment?_____

HOW MUCH TO SEEK EMPLOYMENT?

No, we're not joking. Job or career hunting costs money. **Have you set aside enough money to cover these expenses?**

1.   **Technology.** (*WHY?* Professional correspondence with *neat* typing and *without* spelling will be noted…even in this early stage of pre-employment screening.)
     ☹ Computer and/or software for resume writing and correspondence.
     ☹ Typewriter or rental at copy centers (for evil application packets.)
     ☹ Copy costs (resumes and correspondence should be on matching paper of 20# paper or heavier.)

2.   **Official documents.** (*WHY?* Then, you're paying for the cost of the supporting documents for your background check, not the prospective employer.)
     ★ **Military documents:** DD-214, especially re service and discharge.
     ★ **College transcripts:** (*WHY?* To save the employer from paying background check costs.) "Official" transcripts must be sent by the college and, usually, paid for by you. "Unofficial" transcripts can be supplied by you. Check with your college: you should be entitled to 1-5 *free* unofficial transcripts.

3.   **Travel costs.** (***WHY?*** The prospective employer is not required to pay your travel expenses until *after* you're hired.) You may have to pay for:
   ◎ Airfare/gasoline
   ◎ Motel/hotel if overnight accommodations are recommended or required.
   ◎ Meals.

4.   **Dress for success.** (***WHY?*** You don't get a second chance to make a first impression.) Whether a female or male applicant, you will need:
   💧 A good suit or blazer;
   💧 Dress pants (at least *pressed* twill or non-khaki/non-jean pants);
   💧 Dress shoes (preferably ones with a shine. No kidding! ***WHY?*** Many employers consider unshined shoes evidence of an unprofessional attitude.)
   💧 Appropriate outer attire. (***WHY?*** Picture this: a professionally-dressed employee, wearing a sporting team jacket and cap. If you don't want to spend the money, remove the attire the minute you enter the building or leave it in your vehicle.)

5.   **Fees.**
   💧 *Non*-refundable application fees can run $25 and up *per* position!
   💧 Psychological testing can be extra.
   💧 Any appeal of psychological or medical testing requires *you* to pay for a second test, usually from an approved (and expensive) professional.

SELF-ASSESSMENT: is it the *financial* right time to seek employment? YES/NO
💧 If it isn't the right *financial* time to seek employment, what actions do you have to take now?

_____

_____

☯ When *would* you be ready to seek employment?_____

HOW DO YOU SET AN EMPLOYMENT GOAL?

Until now, you have been diligently analyzing and assessing your goal of seeking employment in your *dream* occupation. Now, honestly and accurately evaluate your self-assessments.

Is your choice of *dream* occupation also a *realistic* employment goal?

☺ You want a career rather than a job.
☺ Your personality is appropriate for your occupational choice.
☺ Your insiders are supportive of you and your occupational choice.
☺ Where you are seeking employment is appropriate for you and attainable by you.
☺ Now is an appropriate time in your personal life to seek employment.
☺ Now is an appropriate time in your professional life to seek employment.
☺ You have enough money set aside for expected expenses.

 **SUMMATION OF SELF-ASSESSMENTS**

◎ **I'm right on target: my occupational dream IS also a realistic employment goal!**
Congratulations! Now, skip to the "Sample Analysis and Assessment Plan" on this
page and learn how to set *realistic* goals and time-frames for achieving your choice of
occupation!

💣 **I'm off-target: my occupational dream is NOT a realistic employment goal!**
Don't despair. It's true: fine-tuning aspirations is stressful and time-intensive. But, it
is more *appropriate* and less stressful in the long-run to honestly and accurately re-
evaluate your occupational choice *now*, than *after* you've gone through the time,
expense and stress of being hired.

   ✂ **Cut out the hopeless feelings**. You are neither hopeless nor helpless. You just
need to re-evaluate your previous, tentative, occupational goal.

   ☎ **Call a friend: you've worked hard and deserve a break.** Clear the cobwebs
from your thinking. You are *not* under any time restraints. Re-evaluating your
occupational goals can wait until tomorrow.

   ◎ **Target your self-assessments.** What worked? *WHY* did they work? What
didn't work? *WHY* didn't they work? How can those areas be improved?

   ☑ **Re-work and re-evaluate your problematic assessment areas.** Only you can
determine which of the areas can and should be re-worked.

 SAMPLE ANALYSIS AND ASSESSMENT PLAN

Review the following sample analysis. Would this analysis help YOU write an
employment plan?

OCCUPATIONAL CHOICE: "I want to be a police officer."

    SHORT-TERM GOAL: Improve overall physical fitness.

    TIME-FRAME: Start as soon as possible. **(YOU define YOUR time frames.)**

        TASK #1: Get physical fitness evaluation from doctor.

        TASK #2: Gauge current level of fitness.

        TASK #3: Prioritize areas of improvement.

        TASK #4: Write physical fitness plan.

        TASK #5: Have plan checked by doctor or <u>qualified</u> fitness trainer.

        TASK #6: Decide fitness equipment needed.

        TASK #7: Set aside space for fitness equipment.

        TASK #8: Purchase fitness equipment still needed.

        TASK #9: Start physical fitness program.

    MID-TERM GOAL: Finish college degree.

    TIME-FRAME: 2 years/3-4 semesters

        TASK #1: Make appointment with counselor re degree status.

        TASK #2: Map out completion of degree.

        TASK #3: Check grants and financial aid re completion of degree.

        TASK #4: Schedule classes still needed.

        TASK #5: Speak with employer re schedule to accommodate courses still needed for graduation.

        TASK #5: Speak with family re work and education schedule.

        TASK #6: Start on last courses still needed.

        TASK #7: Update graduation paperwork per semester.

        TASK #8: Schedule check with counselor before last year of college.

        TASK #9: Apply for graduation.

        TASK #10: Graduate with Grade Point Average of B or higher.

    LONG-TERM GOAL: Obtain police officer position with department who has an academy. (If have to pay for academy, add 5 steps:

        1) research area police academies;

        2) apply to 1-2 academies;

        3) save $3,000 or obtain financial aid;

        4) alter work schedule, as needed;

        5) complete academy, finishing toward top of class.

    TIME-FRAME: Hired within 1 year, start process 3 semesters before graduation. (Hiring takes approximately 6-9 months.)

        TASK #1: Continue fitness routine: add parts from prospective employer's obstacle course and physical fitness test.

        TASK #2: Make list of potential departments, 3 county radius.

        TASK #3: Telephone and check website re hiring.

        TASK #4: Make list of past jobs--duties, supervisors, time frames, wages.

        TASK #5: Download website applications.

        TASK #6: Write and re-write draft of job application.

TASK #7: Write resume, immediately before applying for positions.

TASK #8: Contact references, tell about positions, obtain permission to use their names on application packets.

TASK #9: Apply for positions.

TASK #10: Draft "thank you for interview" letter.

TASK #11: Approaching interview, research department on-line.

TASK #12: Visit department: note drive-time; appearance of building; demeanor of personnel.

TASK #13: Immediately send "thank you" letter after interview.

TASK #14: Decide pro's and con's of accepting position.

TASK #15: Send letter thanking for position or rejecting position, but thanking Chief for employment offer.

YOUR ANALYSIS AND ASSESSMENT PLAN

OCCUPATIONAL CHOICE: "I want to be a _____."

SHORT-TERM GOAL:_____

TIME-FRAME: _____

      TASK #1: _____

      TASK #2: _____

      TASK #3: _____

      TASK #4: _____

      TASK #5: _____

      TASK #6: _____

      TASK #7: _____

      TASK #8: _____

      TASK #9: _____

      TASK #10: _____

MID-TERM GOAL:_____

TIME-FRAME: _____

      TASK #1: _____

      TASK #2: _____

      TASK #3: _____

      TASK #4: _____

      TASK #5: _____

      TASK #6: _____

      TASK #7: _____

      TASK #8: _____

      TASK #9: _____

      TASK #10: _____

LONG-TERM GOAL:_____

TIME-FRAME: _____

      TASK #1: _____

      TASK #2: _____

      TASK #3: _____

      TASK #4: _____

      TASK #5: _____

      TASK #6: _____

      TASK #7: _____

      TASK #8: _____

TASK #9: _____

TASK #10: _____

SELF-ASSESSMENT: is it the *best* time to seek employment? YES/NO

♦* If it isn't the *best* time to seek employment, what actions do you have to take now?

_____

_____

☯ When *would* you be ready to seek employment?_____

CONCLUSION

"The four steps that comprise the career development process are (1) self-assessment, (2) career exploration, (3) job search skill development and (4) implementation of job search steps" (Harr & Hess, 2003, p. 86). In this chapter, you have diligently worked on the final stages of "self-assessment". You first combined the results of your personal assessment (from chapter 1) with your professional preferences (chapter 2). Then, you performed a "series of activities" toward your goal of a realistic career choice by answering the logical questions associated with any systematic, employment plan: *what* is desired, a job or career; *who* is involved; *where* and *when* to seek employment; *how much* is the employment process going to cost; and, finally, *how* do you establish a career goal through an analysis and assessment plan?

For the curious, "career exploration" occurred by using the structured interview (Chapter 2) and then exploring either the law enforcement or corrections chapters. "Job search skill development" was initially addressed under the more criminal justice-style title of "testing chapters". This development process will be completed after you've absorbed basic employment rights (Chapter 10), written a "riveting resume" (Chapter 11), and investigated "interesting interviews" (Chapter 12). Then, all you have to do is successfully "implement your job search steps" and, presto, you've got a career! (Piece of cake!)

One last word to the wise, follow Lore's advice (1998, p. 172): "Manage your Goals List. Revisit your goals often."

SUGGESTED READING

Stay sane during your planning stages: join an association. Visit Directory of Associations at http://www. marketingsource. com/ associations

Research sources for re-entry college students. Visit http://www.back2college.com

REFERENCES

Brown, D., & Brooks, L. (1991). *Career counseling techniques.* Needham Heights, MA: Allyn and Bacon.

Harr, J. S., & Hess, K. M. (2003). *Seeking employment in criminal justice and related fields.* Belmont, CA: Wadsworth/Thomson Learning.

Lore, N. (1998). *The pathfinder:* How to choose or change your career for a lifetime of satisfaction and success. New York, NY: Fireside.

CHAPTER 10

LEGAL LIABILITIES

"From now on we shall offer police jobs to qualified women regardless of sex."
-A New Jersey town's affirmative action statement

AFTER READING THIS CHAPTER, YOU SHOULD KNOW
⇨ What Federal laws prohibit job discrimination.
⇨ What is "sexual harassment" in the workplace.
⇨ What "age discrimination" has to do with your career plans.
⇨ What role "The Americans with Disabilities Act" plays in the hiring process.
⇨ Why you should know about Ohio Civil Service laws.
⇨ What topics employers should avoid during the interview stage.
⇨ What you should do if you believe you've experienced job discrimination.

INTRODUCTION

You're probably asking yourself, "What does this stuff have to do with getting a criminal justice job?" The answer: "MUCH!" No, this is not a law book: the chapter only outlines the basic information about civil rights, job discrimination and employment law. YES, you should definitely read this chapter. No one has the right to discriminate against you and you don't have to accept job discrimination. Bottom line: if you don't read this chapter, how do you know if your prospective employer is obeying the laws? Why would you want to start a job or career with an employer who violates your rights and the law?

FEDERAL LAWS PROHIBITING JOB DISCRIMINATION

According to the Ohio Civil Rights Commission (n.d.), important federal acts which detail prohibitions against job discrimination are: ADA/1990 Americans with Disabilities Act;

ADEA/Age Discrimination Act 1975; Civil Rights Acts of 1964 and 1991. In order, and in accordance with the United States Equal Employment Opportunity Commission (n.d.), **these acts prohibit (or answer questions about) regarding:**

1. Sexual Harassment
2. Race/Color Discrimination
3. Age Discrimination
4. National Origin Discrimination
5. Pregnancy Discrimination
6. Religious Discrimination
7. Americans with Disabilities
8. Sexual Orientation
9. Status as a Parent
10. Marital Status
11. Political Affiliation

SEXUAL HARASSMENT

NO! Sexual harassment does not only happen to women! (Oops, we just helped you answer the first question. Well, you know you'll get more than one of the following questions correct.) Without using the United States Employment Opportunity Commission (n.d.) "Facts About Sexual Harassment", **what is true about sexual harassment? TRUE OR FALSE:**

_____ 1. Only a woman can be a victim of sexual harassment.

_____ 2. The victim has to be the opposite sex from the harasser.

_____ 3. Only the victim's supervisor can harass the employee.

_____ 4. The behavior needs to be "hands-on" to be considered harassment.

_____ 5. Anyone affected by the offensive conduct can file an anti-sexual harassment charge.

_____ 6. The behavior is sexual harassment if it "unreasonably interferes" with the individual's work performance.

_____ 7. The victim needs to be fired or demoted for sexual harassment to have occurred.

_____ 8. "It's only sexual harassment if you don't like it."

117.

☺ **How did you do?**

FALSE 1. **NO:** a man can also be a victim of sexual harassment.

FALSE 2. The victim **does not** have to be the opposite sex from the harasser.

FALSE 3. **NOT** only can the victim's supervisor harass the employee, but according to the United States Equal Employment Opportunity Commission (n.d.), so can "an agent of the employer, a supervisor in another area, a co-worker, or a non-employee."

FALSE 4. The behavior does **not** need to be "hands-on" to be considered harassment. Per the United States Equal Employment Opportunity Commission (n.d.): "Unwelcome sexual advances, requests for sexual favors, and other verbal or physical conduct of a sexual nature constitutes sexual harassment…."

TRUE 5. Anyone affected by the offensive conduct can file an anti-sexual harassment charge. The person just needs to be affected by the "offensive" conduct.

TRUE 6. The behavior is sexual harassment if it "unreasonably interferes" with the individual's work performance or "creates an intimidating, hostile or offense work environment" [The United States Equal Employment Opportunity Commission (n.d.).]

FALSE 7. The victim need **not** be fired or demoted for sexual harassment to have occurred. "Unlawful sexual harassment may occur without economic injury to or discharge of the victim" [The United States Equal Employment Opportunity Commission (n.d.).]

TRUE 8. "It's only sexual harassment if you don't like it." According to the United States Equal Employment Opportunity Commission (n.d.): "(t)he harasser's conduct must be unwelcome."

AGE DISCRIMINATION

"…(N)o person in the United States shall, on the basis of age, be excluded from participation, (sic) in be denied the benefits of, or be subjected to discrimination under, any program or activity receiving Federal financial assistance." (Age Discrimination Act of 1975, 42 U.S.C. Sections 6101-6107). So, sounds as though any criminal justice agency receiving federal funds can't prohibit you from applying for the position because of your age. That's basically correct…unless the agency can prove that age is a bona fide occupation qualification. In other words, if the agency can prove that your age will prohibit you from effectively performing the critical tasks of your job (the bona fide occupational qualifications), you can still be eliminated because you're too old. Rats.

1990 AMERICANS WITH DISABILTIES ACT

According to Harr & Hess (2003, p. 94): "The Americans with Disabilities Act (ADA) prohibits medical examinations or inquiries regarding mental or physical problems or disabilities *before* a conditional offer of employment has been made." While the physical agility test can be administered anytime within the hiring process, a medical *exam* cannot unless the employer says you're hired if you pass the *medical exam.* If you're not sure whether you are covered under this act, contact the Ohio Civil Rights Commission, United States Equal Employment Opportunity Commission or Ohio Attorney General's Civil Rights and/or Employment Law sections.

OHIO CIVIL SERVICE LAW

According to Downes & Albrecht (2001, p. 213), "O.R.C. (Ohio Revised Code) 737.11 mandates that the police departments of every city shall be maintained under the civil service system. Therefore, vacancies in the classified service of police departments must…use…competitive examination." So, Ohio Civil Service law includes how the hiring and promotional process, eligibility list, longevity of the list. If any inconsistencies, irregularities or violations occur, there are set procedures for the Ohio Civil Service Commission to investigate. You may be restricted to certain steps and procedures within the system; but, you will have a system and, if necessary, a means of appeal violations.

LAWFUL & UNLAWFUL TOPICS

The following information is general. For further details, visit the Ohio Civil Rights Commission at http://www.state.oh.us/crc

	LAWFUL TOPICS	UNLAWFUL TOPICS
1. EMPLOYEE'S DEMOGRAPHICS	☺ **NAME** ☺ **ADDRESS** ☺ **PHOTOGRAPH ID** ☯ **AGE** (*if* minimum age required by law) ☯ **HEIGHT/WEIGHT** (*if* job-related) ☯ **DISABILITY** (*if* re ability to substantially perform specific job) ☯ **CITIZENSHIP** (*after* being hired) ☺ **RELATIVES** (*re* emergency notification)	💣 **USING ANY OF THESE TOPICS TO AS A SNEAKY AND ILLEGAL INQUIRY INTO RACE, COLOR, RELIGION, SEX, NATIONAL ORIGIN, HANDICAP, AGE OR ANCESTRY**
2. EMPLOYEE'S BACKGROUND	☺ **EDUCATION** ☺ **LANGUAGES** (*if* job-related skill) ☺ **WORK HISTORY** ☺ **VOCATIONAL TRAINING** ☺ **MILITARY SERVICE** ☯ **CONVICTIONS** (*if* re to job qualifications)	💣 **SAME AS ABOVE** 💣 **ARRESTS** (*without* convictions)
3. QUALIFICATIONS	☺ **WORK SCHEDULE** (when available) ☺ **QUALIFICATIONS** ☺ **REFERENCES**	💣 **SAME AS ABOVE & if unlawful inquiry into marital status and children (sex discrimination).**

RESPONDING TO JOB DISCRIMINATION

Talk about an explosive situation! No one should have to suffer job discrimination: your government passed laws and acts to protect you as much as possible against this job-related stressor. But, in reality, there is probably an unlawful question being asked of a criminal justice applicant even as you're reading this page.

Before choosing one of the following responses, ask yourself three questions:
◎ **WHAT IS THE MOTIVATION?** Is the interviewer asking the question out of ignorance or as an act of discrimination?

◎ **IS THE INTERVIEWER AN ANOMALY?** Yes, the interviewer is so high up the chain of command as to have interviewing and/or hiring authority. But, does the interviewer typify standard organizational culture and behavior? Do YOU want to be associated with an organization which condones such ignorance and/or illegal activity?

◎ **HOW MUCH DO I WANT THE JOB?** Are you willing to ignore the unlawful question and situation occur or is this the point beyond which you will not go?

The following are possible responses for YOU, if you believe you've been a victim of job discrimination:

🏳 **IGNORANCE:** Pretend it didn't happen and ignore the question.

🏳 **CONFUSED BUT POLITE:** This response gives the interviewer a chance to correct the unlawful question and helps you determine whether the motivation was ignorance or discrimination. EXAMPLE: "I'm not sure what information you want. Could you please rephrase the question?"

🏳 **CONCERNED BUT STILL PROFESSIONAL:** If you feel the interviewer needs to be aware of the unlawful question; but, you are still trying to determine motivation. EXAMPLE: "Could you please explain how this question relates to <u>(the job for which you're applying)</u> ?"

🏳 **CONCERNED BUT LESS PROFESSIONAL:** EXAMPLE: "Would you explain how this question relates to <u>(the job for which you're applying)</u> ?" (No "please".)

💣 **EXTREMELY SERIOUS:** This response puts the interviewer on notice for having committed unlawful, job-related discrimination; but, still allows a small chance to correct the error. WARNING: while you have every right to be upset by an unlawful hiring question, a more decisive response such as this one could be interpreted as belligerence and be detrimental to your hiring prospects. EXAMPLE: "Isn't that an unlawful interviewing question?"

☎ **FILING A COMPLAINT:** Again, while you should not suffer job discrimination, legal action on your part has ramifications. Yes, as a result of winning your job action, you could force the agency to redress (correct) their procedures, earn a financial settlement and/or the position your originally sought. But, review the Ohio Civil Rights Commission Complaint Procedures, first, before making your decision to file a complaint. This is a protracted legal battle. Are you prepared for a stressful, long-term commitment with personal, familial, professional and financial consequences? If so, file the complaint. If not, walk away: be proud of your ethical standards and grateful you didn't accept a position with such an unprofessional--and/or unlawful--criminal justice organization.

CONCLUSION

As the saying goes, "Good things come in small packages." This may have been a relatively short chapter, but you reviewed both the Federal and Ohio laws prohibiting job discrimination, particularly relating to sexual harassment, age and disability discrimination. While the interview process will be more comprehensively addressed in Chapter 11, we thought it more appropriate to address lawful and unlawful interviewing inquiries and the wide spectrum of responses to unlawful inquiries, here. The three questions you considered when faced with job discrimination hold true for the entire hiring process: (1) What is the motivation? (Why is the organization requiring this question or step in the hiring process?) (2) Is the unusual situation and/or illegal activity an anomaly, abnormal? (3) How much do I want this job...or career? Am I willing to accept--and, by acquiescence, condone--such behavior in my employer?

SUGGESTED READING

Research Ohio civil rights and employment law at the Ohio Attorney General's website at http://www.ag. state.oh.us/

Investigate Ohio, Federal and international civil and human rights-related documents via the Ohio Civil Rights Commission website at http://www.state.oh.us/crc

Research Federal anti-job discrimination laws and procedures at the United States Equal Employment Opportunity Commission website: http://www.eeoc.gov/eeoinfo.html

REFERENCES

Age Discrimination Act of 1975. (1975). *42 U.S.C., Section 6102. Prohibition of discrimination.* Retrieved October 24, 2002, from Ohio Civil Rights Commission, http://www.state.oh.us/crc/documents/age1975.htm

Downes, J. J. & Albrecht, B. S. (2001). Legal considerations for entry level hiring. In *The complete guide to hiring law enforcement officers* (pp. 2 -2). Columbus, OH: Law Enforcement Foundation, Inc.

Harr, J. S. & Hess, K. M. (2003). *Seeking employment in criminal justice and related fields.* Belmont, CA: Wadsworth/Thomson Learning.

Ohio Civil Rights Commission. (n.d.). *Civil and human rights related documents.* Retrieved October 24, 2002, from http://www.state.oh.us/crc/Documents.htm

Ohio Civil Rights Commission. (n.d.). *Ohio civil rights commission complaint procedure.* Retrieved October 24, 2002, from http://www.state.oh.us/crc/ ocrccomp.html

The United States Equal Employment Opportunity Commission. (n.d.). *Facts about employment discrimination.* Retrieved October 24, 2002, from http://www.eeoc. gov/eeoinfo.html

The United States Equal Employment Opportunity Commission. (n.d.). *Facts about sexual harassment.* Retrieved October 24, 2002, from http://www.eeoc. gov/facts/fs-sex.html

CHAPTER 11

RESONATING RESUMES

I read part of it all the way through. -MGM's Samuel Goldwyn

AFTER READING THIS CHAPTER, YOU SHOULD KNOW
- ⇨ What the employer wants.
- ⇨ What are transferable traits.
- ⇨ Why format follows function.
- ⇨ What information to include (and exclude).
- ⇨ How to get organized.
- ⇨ What action verbs are and how to use them.
- ⇨ How to reduce resume redundancy.
- ⇨ What should be included in the first draft of a resume.
- ⇨ What should be included in the final draft of a resume.
- ⇨ What a cover letter should cover.

INTRODUCTION

The criminal justice field is a practical one. We prefer lists rather than text, case studies rather than abstracts. Therefore, resumes geared toward the criminal justice field should also be practical and, as you already learned in Chapter 10, succinct.

You must consider that the reviewer of your resume to be very much like the above picture. The reviewer is blind to your strengths (and weaknesses) until reading your resume and only knows what you want the reviewer to know. Consequently, your resume must resonate with your strengths and blatantly sign your praises as an efficient, effective employee. Remember: the resume stage may be your only chance to get your foot in the criminal justice door: choose your words carefully, accurately and succinctly!

Let's begin by examining what the employer and you, the prospective employee want. Then, we'll assist you, step-by-step, to build a succinct, redundant-free, criminal justice-based resume!

WHAT DOES THE EMPLOYER WANT?

Didn't we already answer this question? Yes, from one perspective, we did already address this issue in Chapter 2, when we examined picking a "good" employer. But, in Chapter 2, we addressed **your** needs, which don't necessarily match those of an employer.

"Organizational politics refer to the practice of using means other than merit or good performance for…gaining favor in the organization" (Rue, L. W., & Byars, L. L., 1996, pp. 68-69). In other words, keeping your boss happy means supporting organizational politics, while you reduce the likelihood of being fired. Let's adapt a few of their suggestions for keeping your boss happy to our discussion here. **Can you answer "yes" to the following questions?**

★ Are you loyal to the organizations you've worked for?
★ Do you avoid antagonizing other employees and departments?
★ Do you show respect to other employees and supervisors?
★ Have you gained the respect of subordinates?
★ Do you seek responsibility and remain accountable for your actions?
★ Do you socialize with other members of the organization?

What do these questions have to do with a resume? Simple: the reviewer of your resume will be carefully scrutinizing your resume to see if these positive traits resonate from your carefully chosen words and phrases. For example, let's re-examine these questions from an **employer's** perspective:

★ **Are you loyal to the organizations you've worked for?**
    Resume: How long have you stayed in each of your jobs? Can your resignations or reasons for leaving those jobs be logically explained or are they non-employer-friendly? For example: did you leave because you accepted a better position or returned to school? On the other hand, did you leave because you were fired, didn't get along with the boss, weren't promoted, etc…?

★ **Do you avoid antagonizing other employees and departments?**
    Resume: Does your phrasing sound more like bragging or a list of accomplishments? (For example, did you "assist in" or "single-handedly complete" a project? Again, why did you leave your other employment? Are any of your former supervisors willing to be references for your resume and/or application?

125.

★ **Do you show respect to other employees and supervisors?**

Resume: Do you take credit for being a team-player? Have you won any awards for "Outstanding Employee"? Do you mention being able to work with people from diverse backgrounds? Do you "handle complaints" or "deal with difficult people"? (Preferably, your resume indicates the former, not the latter!)

★ **Have you gained the respect of subordinates?**

Resume: Have you reduced shrinkage (theft)? Has your team earned a reward? Have you moved progressively and reasonably up the promotional ladder? (The **theory** here is that only an effective employee and supervisor will continue to be promoted.) A supervisor can only truly gain the respect of subordinates by **earning** it: respect which is not earned is coercive and tied only to the title of the position, **not** the person who fills that position. So, in the interview process (more than here, in the resume process), a prospective employer will note whether you shift blame or take undue credit for a team's accomplishment. Either response exemplifies a level of disrespect toward your subordinates, intimating your failure to have **earned** their respect in the first place.

★ **Do you seek responsibility and remain accountable for your actions?**

Resume: Seeking responsibility can be demonstrated by being trusted to open and close a business, handle cash, manage people and accounts and be promoted through the ranks. Being accountable is easier to highlight in the application and interview processes, especially through the examination of stated reasons for leaving an employer or position of responsibility.

★ **Do you socialize with other members of the organization?**

Resume: What trade or business associations do you list on your resume? Have you ever been elected or volunteered for a position of leadership in those associations? Have you won or earned an award in any of those associations?

Chief Patrick Oliver (2001, pp. 50-51) listed twelve selection criteria for law enforcement officer candidates. In a discussion about resumes, four new criterion are pertinent:

☞ **Can the candidate effectively communicate in writing?**

Resume: Is the resume logical, succinct and easy to read? Is it grammatically correct and free of spelling errors?

☞ **Can the candidate demonstrate a team orientation?**

Resume: Good for you! Yes, we did already do this one. Just checking to see if you're on your toes! An effective candidate can also think on his or her feet!

☞ **Does the candidate have planning and organizing skills?**

Resume: Do you? For instance, do you logically and reasonably have a heading for planning or organizational skills? Any scheduling of staff, training, events etc...? Were you ever a project manager? A supervisor? How *many* activities or people did you organize at any given time? (Here, the largest number which can be supported by witnesses or documents is preferable.)

☞ **Is the candidate performance driven?**

    Resume: Did you ever complete a project under deadline? Have you exhibited time management skills relating to staffing, scheduling, documentation? **Careful**: don't ignore this criteria. This whole question intimates an ability to survive under stressful conditions and excel in time management. This does **so** apply to criminal justice! Think about the time management skills involved in completing a criminal investigation; generating an annual report on departmental shrinkage activities; sending in your agency's <u>Uniform Crime Report</u> statistics; preparing for court (police-related, probation or parole violation); staffing a shift; scheduling prison activities; scheduling a civic tour of the jail so it does **not** coincide with inmate activities; finishing a pre-sentence report for a juvenile adjudication hearing; etc....

Chief Wayne I. McCoy (2001) discussed a sample job task analysis: a comprehensive list of tasks completed by an individual in a certain position, prioritized by demand, importance and frequency (p. 79). From this discussion we can add that an employer would be examining a resume to see if three additional criteria exist:

☑ **Supervisory Skills**: Does the resume indicate any behaviors relating to recruiting; hiring; staffing; scheduling; supervising; discipline employees?

☑ **Managerial Skills**: Any phrasing or headings relating multi-tasking, prioritizing and organizing demands on resources?

☑ **Interpersonal Skills**: Does the resume include statements about communicating with people, agencies or the general public? Any reference to explaining procedures, handling complaints, processing public needs?

WHAT ARE TRANSFERABLE SKILLS?

Basically, transferable skills "transfer" from one employer or employment field to another because virtually every job or career needs and/or values these "universal" skills. Consequently, when starting (or changing) a career, the person who can demonstrate the most transferable skills will be favored by the prospective employer.

✓ **Which of the following transferable skills do you have?**

☺ Written communication skills (interoffice memorandum, letters, reports, etc....)
☺ Oral communication skills (appropriate responses re small & large group discussions)
☺ Math skills (especially re shrinkage/losses and reports)
☺ Reasoning (and research) skills
☺ Supervisory (includes teaching and leadership) skills
☺ Interpersonal/human relations-related skills
☺ Cultural perspective (knowledge, experience and/or empathy re diverse cultures)
☺ Self-discipline (includes perseverance)
☺ Self-confidence (without being over-confident and/or condescending)
☺ Imagination (includes creative problem solving skills)
☺ Insight (or intuition)

FORMAT FOLLOWS FUNCTION

The key to an effective resume is choosing the format which most closely matches the résumé's function. **Review the following table and *then* the next two pages.**

	GOAL?	**YOUR WORK EXPERIENCE?**	☹ **FORMAT'S WEAKNESSES?**
CHRONO-LOGICAL	Advance within present company or occupation	Strong work experience emphasized	Emphasizes past work/duties, **not** transferable skills & duties; redundancy
FUNCTIONAL	Changing career **or** re-entry to job market	Includes part-time & volunteer work. Lack of work experience **de-emphasized**	If poorly written, can be viewed as "fluff" or "lying"
COMBINATION	Changing careers	Strong work experience but indirectly re to new occupation	Non-standard, hard to organize, may create annoying redundancy

128.

EXAMPLE, CHRONOLOGICAL RESUME

JOHN Q. SMITH
2792 Forestview Avenue
Rocky River, Ohio 44116
Home: 440-331-1234
Work: 440-987-6543

EDUCATION:

B.A.-Criminal Justice, 2002.
Any Name College, City, State.
- Courses in sociology, psychology, criminology, delinquency, government, communication, humanities.
- 3 times Dean's List, 3.67 Cumulative GPA
- AKA Sociology Honorary

TECHNICAL EXPERIENCE:

XYZ County Correctional Facility; 1234 State Rd.; City, OH 44123. Correctional Officer II (Fall, 1998-Present): Conducted building security; scheduled, supervised 3-5 officers/shift; monitored pod of 22 inmates; wrote reports; supervised 15-30 visitors per week; reviewed & responded to incidents; performed self-defense and first aid, as needed.

ABC Juvenile Detention Home; 567 River Ave.; City, OH 44098. Correctional Officer (Summer, 1997): Conducted security for pod; monitored pod of 12 inmates; wrote reports; supervised 10-15 visitors per week; responded to incidents; performed self-defense and first aid.

CDF Hospital; 789 County Rd.; City, OH 44094. Hospital Aide Volunteer (Part-time, Aug.-May 1997): Assisted staff with hospital and social events; worked with 25 patients in "Special Friends" mentoring program; coordinated and publicized 2 nationally-recognized, guest speakers; performed first-aid.

OTHER EXPERIENCE:

Bank One; 678 Erie St.; City, OH 44060. Bank Teller (1995-1997): Managed cash drawer of $3,000; performed customer service; assisted in annual audit; used income to finance 75% of educational costs.

AFFILIATIONS:

ABC Sheriff's Department Explorer's Post #123.
Rocky River City Blockwatch Program (Elected block captain).
Junior League, Rocky River City.

EXAMPLE, FUNCTIONAL RESUME

JOHN Q. SMITH
2792 Forestview Avenue
Rocky River, Ohio 44116
Home: 440-331-1234
Work: 440-987-6543

SUMMARY OF QUALIFICATIONS

ORGANIZATION/ADMINISTRATION
- Supervised, trained and disciplined 5 officers.
- Scheduled, staffed and deployed shift of 5 officers.
- Reviewed and analyzed shift responses to correctional incidents.
- Supervised up to 30 visitors per week re safety, security, procedures, and time management requirements.
- Monitored officers and visitors for standard operating procedural compliance.
- Coordinated and publicized 2 nationally-recognized, speaking events.
- Organized, publicized and helped run mentoring program of 25 participants.
- Responsible for $3,000 cash drawer.
- Performed problem-solving and handled customer complaints, as needed.

CORRECTIONS-RELATED
- Monitored and enforced procedures for pod of 22 inmates.
- Conducted pod and building/perimeter security on hourly basis.
- Responded to correctional incidents.
- Wrote and processed departmental reports.
- Performed self-defense and first aid, as needed.

EDUCATION

B.A.-Criminal Justice	Any Name College; Ohio	2002
	• 12 criminal justice-re courses	
	• Dean's List-3 times & GPA 3.67	
	• AKA Sociology Honorary	

EMPLOYMENT HISTORY

• Correctional Officer II	XYZ County Correctional Facility City, Ohio 44123	Fall, 1998--
• Correctional Officer	ABC Juvenile Detention Home City, Ohio 44098	Summer, 1997
• Volunteer Aide	CDF Hospital; City, Ohio 44094	8-96 to 8-97
• Bank Teller	Bank One; City, Ohio 44060	1995-1997

INFORMATION TO INCLUDE

1. CONTACT INFORMATION	*<u>Name</u> (first, middle, last, NO nicknames); *<u>Mailing</u> address; *<u>Work telephone number</u> (with area code & if can accept calls at work); *<u>Home telephone number</u> w/ area code; *<u>Email</u> (if requested or filing resume electronically).
2. WORK EXPERIENCE	*<u>Part-time</u> (if summer employment or longer than 3+ months); *<u>Full-time</u> (if summer or 3+ months); *<u>Military</u> (any length of service, note branch, grade and type of discharge); *<u>Volunteer-based</u> (any and all service); *<u>Awards</u>; *<u>Certifications/licenses</u> if work related (esp. re teaching academies or repairing equipment--both save employer money) *<u>Publications</u>.
3. EDUCATION	*<u>College</u> (degree, awards & associations); *<u>High School</u> (IF within last 5 years OR if no college experience. See next table); *<u>Training</u> (academies, internships, schools 1 or more weeks in length).
4. COMMUNITY AFFILIATIONS & PROFESSIONAL ASSOCIATIONS	*<u>General membership</u>; *<u>Offices held</u> (note whether elected or volunteered); *<u>Projects</u> managed; *<u>Certifications/licenses</u>; *<u>Awards</u>.
5. SPECIAL SKILLS	*<u>"Foreign" languages</u>; *<u>Computer languages/software</u>; *<u>Martial arts or weaponry</u>; *<u>Motor vehicle repair</u>.

INFORMATION TO EXCLUDE

Don't voluntarily jump off the deep end by including information in your resume which is derogatory, opens you to prejudice and/or discrimination or is better addressed in the interview stage. However, do **not** lie or exaggerate: any negative information and misinformation will be discovered through careful reading of your application or resume and as a result of your background investigation, polygraph or interview. Remember that most application forms have a disclaimer: you lie, you're at least deleted from the prospective employee pool and, you may even be summarily discharged. It's not worth the risk, just be prepared to address the potentially damaging information in Chapter 12: Interesting Interview!

ISSUE/INFORMATION TO DELETE	WHY *NOT* INCLUDE ON RESUME?
1. PICTURE	Can lead to bias or discrimination.
2. OBJECTIVE	Redundant by application or cover letter.
3. DEMOGRAPHIC INFORMATION	*Race, gender, religion, political affiliation issues can cause bias or discrimination. *Remember high school, previous table? Graduation dates could open you to age discrimination. Unless there's an age cutoff for application, do not include. *Health by law is addressed either through physical agility tests (job-related only) or conditional offer of employment. See Chapter 10.)
4. DEROGATORY INFORMATION	*Debt determined from background check. *Firing in application and interview. *Employment gaps self-evident by employment dates. Address 3+ months in interview. See Chapter 12.) *Health will exclude you from the start or answerable in agility or conditional offer of employment stages.
5. REFERENCES	Redundant by application & wastes space. Include only if requested.

GETTING ORGANIZED

The key to unlocking the information in your brain and for your resume is logic. You've analyzed your skav's (remember your skills, knowledge, abilities and values from Chapters 1 & 2?) and decided whether you are more interested in law enforcement (Chapters 3 through 5) or corrections (Chapters 7-8). Now, you need to put it all together. Do not panic. Just be logical and start a page or folder for each of the following steps:

#1-TITLE: Review the examples & write down **your** information.

#2-WORK: **Each** job (part- or full-time, paid or volunteer) gets **one** worksheet.

#3-EDUCATION: **Each** degree, certification, license and **important** school gets **one** worksheet.
Degrees: Associates, Bachelors, Masters, Doctorate
Schools Academies, military, agency- or government-sponsored seminar or schools of one week or more.
Certifications/Licenses: anything Ohio Peace Officer Training Council; State of Ohio; Attorney General.

#4-COMMUNITY AFFILIATIONS: If you serve as project coordinator, officer (elected or volunteer then, one worksheet. Otherwise, list the correct spelling and full name of the affiliations. If you don't belong to a community organization, consider joining one. Look in your yellow pages under a special interest, i.e. American Red Cross, animal protective leagues, associations, crisis centers, religious institutions, United Way, etc....

#5-PROFESSIONAL ASSOCIATIONS: Keep a list of the associations or use one worksheet per association for which you hold an office. You need to demonstrate to a prospective employer you're realistic, dedicated and have a long-term perspective toward your degree and the criminal justice field. Review associations In the yellow pages or try Directory of Associations at http://ww.marketing source.com/associations.

ACTUALLY USING ACTION VERBS

One of the biggest hurdles in writing your first resume draft is choosing the correct verb tense and, then, the appropriate verb. By using the **past tense**, you are not only stating the highlights of your past, employment-related accomplishments, you are also suggesting you can demonstrate the same skills, knowledge and abilities in the future. In other words, you're emphasizing to the prospective employer your proven work record.

The **appropriate verb** is one which closely explains the accomplishment or event, without having a negative connotation or exaggerating the action. For instance, review the resume examples. In the chronological resume, our candidate "worked with 25 patients in 'Special Friends' mentoring program." But, in our functional resume, our candidate "Organized, publicized and helped run mentoring program of 25 participants." As the prospective employer, who would you prefer to hire?

☑ **Check the following list of active verbs. How many of them apply to your employment history?** (Circle the verbs or make a list to use on your worksheets.)

*Administered	*Distributed	*Persuaded
*Advised	*Edited	*Planned
*Analyzed	*Evaluated	*Prepared
*Anticipated	*Examined	*Processed
*Appraised	*Exhibited	*Promoted
*Arranged	*Facilitated	*Protected
*Assembled	*Initiated	*Published
*Assisted	*Inspected	*Recruited
*Budgeted	*Interpreted	*Repaired
*Classified	*Interviewed	*Represented
*Coached	*Investigated	*Researched
*Collected	*Managed	*Reviewed
*Compiled	*Mediated	*Rewrote
*Constructed	*Mentored	*Sold
*Controlled	*Monitored	*Spoke
*Coordinated	*Motivated	*Supervised
*Counseled	*Negotiated	*Taught
*Created	*Observed	*Translated
*Delegated	*Obtained	*Troubleshoot
*Designed	*Operated	*Updated
*Developed	*Organized	*Wrote

134.

EMPLOYMENT WORKSHEET

DIRECTIONS: Use one worksheet for each part- & full-time, military & volunteer job. For duties, imagine one day at work and list EACH task completed for EACH job performed during that day.

Employer's Name _____
Employer's Address _____
_____

Employer's Phone   (____)_____ FAX_____
My Title _____ Dates_____
Supervisor's Name/Title_____
Duties: _____
_____
_____
_____
_____
_____
_____
_____
_____
_____
_____

Special Training (government-sponsored or 1+ week):_____
_____
_____
_____

Certifications/Licenses:_____
_____
_____

Awards/Citations:_____
_____
_____

Special Projects:_____
_____
_____

Notes/Special Information not already addressed:_____
_____
_____

EMPLOYMENT WORKSHEET

DIRECTIONS: Use one worksheet for each part- & full-time, military & volunteer job. For duties, imagine one day at work and list EACH task completed for EACH job performed during that day.

Employer's Name _____

Employer's Address _____

_____

Employer's Phone (___)_____ FAX_____

My Title _____ Dates_____

Supervisor's Name/Title_____

Duties: _____

_____

_____

_____

_____

_____

_____

_____

_____

_____

_____

Special Training (government-sponsored or 1+ week):_____

_____

_____

_____

Certifications/Licenses:_____

_____

_____

Awards/Citations:_____

_____

_____

Special Projects:_____

_____

_____

Notes/Special Information not already addressed:_____

_____

_____

EMPLOYMENT WORKSHEET

DIRECTIONS: Use one worksheet for each part- & full-time, military & volunteer job. For duties, imagine one day at work and list EACH task completed for EACH job performed during that day.

Employer's Name _____

Employer's Address _____

_____

Employer's Phone (___) _____ FAX _____

My Title _____ Dates _____

Supervisor's Name/Title_____

Duties: _____

_____

_____

_____

_____

_____

_____

_____

_____

_____

_____

Special Training (government-sponsored or 1+ week):_____

_____

_____

_____

Certifications/Licenses:_____

_____

_____

Awards/Citations:_____

_____

_____

Special Projects:_____

_____

_____

Notes/Special Information not already addressed:_____

_____

_____

EDUCATION WORKSHEET

College: _____

Address: _____

Phone: (___)_____ Years Attended: _____

Degree: _____ Major/Minor: _____

Cumulative GPA: _____ GPA in Degree: _____

Dean's List/Honors: _____

_____

_____

Courses in Degree's Major/Criminal Justice-related Field: _____

_____

_____

_____

_____

_____

_____

XXXXXXXXXXXXXXXXXXXXXXXXXXXXXXXXXXXXXXXXXXXXXXXXXXXXX

EDUCATION WORKSHEET

College/High School: _____

Address: _____

Phone: (___)_____ Years Attended: _____

Degree: _____ Major/Minor: _____

Cumulative GPA: _____ GPA in Degree: _____

Dean's List/Honors: _____

_____

_____

Courses in Degree's Major/Criminal Justice-related Field: _____

_____

_____

_____

_____

_____

_____

COMMUNITY AFFILIATION & PROFESSIONAL ASSOCIATION WORKSHEET

Association's Name _____

Association's Address _____

_____

Association's Phone (___) _____ FAX _____

Association's Email _____

My Title _____ Dates _____

Association is Local, State or National Level: _____

_____

Association's Mission/Purpose: _____

_____

_____

_____

_____

_____

Special Training: _____

_____

_____

Necessary Certifications/Licenses: _____

_____

_____

_____

Awards/Citations: _____

_____

_____

Special Projects: _____

_____

_____

Notes/Special Information not already addressed: _____

_____

_____

_____

REDUCING RESUME REDUNDANCY

A resume is not supposed to be a burden or lengthy tome: it's designed to be succinct. So many applicants apply for each open position: a resume reviewer does not have the luxury of spending minutes carefully examining each resume. Key words and phrases, especially those indicative of a particular field or position, must **leap** out of the page. Redundancy of qualifications, unnecessary wording and incorrect verb usage create a cumbersome resume and reduce reading comprehension.

✤ Consider this scenario. You have two documents in front of you. One document is a well-written, one- to two-page list of carefully chosen statements under logical headings. The other is a multi-page document, redolent with redundancy, without headings. Which would you read? The first document...as will the resume reviewer.

So, follow our suggestions to reduce redundancy:

REDUNDANCY TO REDUCE	WHY THE REDUCTION
1. OVERUSE OF VERB	Results from improper planning: an unfavorable trait in a prospective employee.
2. ERRORS	With grammar- & spell-check, errors are indicative of a lack of thoroughness which could be unfairly applied to how well you'd perform in court or in report writing.
3. FANCY FONTS & COLORS	Hard to read and potentially irritating.
4. NON-QUANTIFIED SKILLS	Lays groundwork for level of skill i.e. if you've supervised 3 people, 4 is not much different; but, 6 could be a stretch.
5. LESSER-INCLUDED SKILLS	Why take credit for supervising 1 person, when you can take credit for 3?
6. PAGES 2+	Unless you have considerable work experience, certifications or memberships, 2+ pages means unnecessary redundancy and poor planning. Think short and sweet: be succinct!

WHAT TO INCLUDE IN THE FIRST DRAFT

Now comes the hard work: pulling the information from this whole chapter together into a succinct, one page document. Remember: a draft is imperfect. Expect to revisit your draft several times and ask the advice of friends and/or family. The **final** draft should be perfect: the **first** draft is just an outline.

To facilitate writing your first draft, follow these steps in the order they're written:

✸ **Review your employment worksheets for quantified skills.** Add the numeric amounts, whenever logical, with either the maximum amount (i.e. "Supervised 3 employees") or a range with time reference (i.e. "Addressed 15-20 customer service requests per week.")

✕ **Delete redundant skill statements.** For example, if you've, "Supervised 3 employees", delete any references to supervising 1-2 employees. If you've, "Addressed 15-20 customer service requests per week", delete any references to addressing less than 20 requests per week or less than 4 requests per day.

☑ **Check and highlight the non-deleted, remaining skill statements.**

⊠ **Write a new list of all remaining skill statements.**

ꖌ **Flag similar skill statements and note similar categories.** For example, do you have a number of skills which could logically be called, "Administration", "Human Relations", "Planning", "Teaching/Training", "Human Resources" or "Organizational"? Hopefully, a "Criminal Justice-Related" category will also emerge.

☺ **Group skill statements under 2-4 categories.** You choose; but, 1 category can look like poor planning and 4,, like "fluff" or exaggeration.

◉ **Target your strengths.** If you have a college degree, but minimal or no criminal-justice-related experience, place your "Education" heading before "Employment History". If you're strong in work-related skills but weak on education, reverse the order and list work first and education, second.

★ **Now, write your draft!** Remember examples have been given for your edification.

FINISHING YOUR FINAL DRAFT

The final draft is a result of tightening your first draft and contacting trusted friends, family members and co-workers. Give **your** reviewer a copy of a job posting and your first draft. Ask the reviewer to use the following checklist to assess the "readability" of your resume:

ITEM TO BE CHECKED	CONCERNS TO ADDRESS
1. PRINT APPEARANCE	+White or off-white paper, 20 pound weight used? (Shows quality and will be easier to scan on computer.) +Printed in black ink? (Easier to read and photocopy.) +Is it in 12 pt type? (Smaller type or italic fonts are harder to read..) +1 page? 2, only IF APPROPRIATE! +Filing electronically? Use ASCII version (text only, no format).
2. HEADINGS	+Bold, capitalized headings used? +Title (name, address, phones) included? +2-4 Qualification headings included? +Qualification headings match skills listed under each heading? Logical order? +Education heading included? +Employment History heading included? +Community Affiliations or Professional Association (if applicable) included? +Publications or Award headings (if applicable) included?
3. READABILITY	+"Easy" on the eye? (Looks great?) +Spacing ok? (If there's space, 3 lines between paragraphs is preferred, 2 lines is acceptable spacing.) +No grammatical nor spelling errors?
4. WORD USAGE	+All personal pronouns deleted? +Each skill statement starts with **action** verb in **past** tense? +Criminal justice terms used?

COVERING COVER LETTERS

A cover letter is critical because it accomplishes two equally important goals. First, a cover letter is the first time the resume reviewer is introduced to you: your philosophies, skills, knowledge, abilities and values. Based on which skill statements you highlight, your semantics and grammar, the reviewer forms a positive or negative first impression of you. Secondly, the cover letter is your only chance to state how your background directly matches the position for which you are applying: a resume is only a check list of your qualifications and not explanatory in nature. So, compose your cover letter carefully: it is your first…and, possibly, your last…chance to make a good impression.

WHAT TO INCLUDE IN YOUR SAMPLE COVER LETTER:

☑ **Optional** but professional. Design your cover letter to match your resume. Type the same heading, address, telephone numbers in the center of your cover letter as you did in the center of the first page of your resume. (Drop down to the 3rd line for the date.)

☑ **Date** but be sure you're under any job opening-deadline. (Drop down to 5th line.)

☑ **Recipient's information** (If possible, do not send the letter, "To Whom It May Concern". **Call** (email may be outdated) the agency and get the correct spelling **and** title of the person receiving resumes. If the add is to an un-named organization, be safe and address the letter to, "Dear Sir/Ma'am:" rather than get the gender wrong.

☑ **1st Paragraph** is the introduction and should include how you learned of the job opening (newspaper, magazine, website, name of person/referral). Be sure to name the exact position for which you're applying: they may have multiple job openings.

☑ **2nd Paragraph** is your chance to shine. Use bullets to highlight your expertise **categories and** how they relate to the position and agency for which you're applying.

☑ **3rd Paragraph** use a strong closure indicating you're a team player and thanking the reviewer for the opportunity to be heard.

☑ **Closure:** "Sincerely", drop down to 4th line, type your legal name. Then, drop another 2 lines and type "Enc" or "Enclosure" to remind the reader of additional pages enclosed in this envelope and yet to be read.

SAMPLE COVER LETTER

JOHN Q. SMITH
2792 Forestview Avenue
Rocky River, Ohio 44116
Home: 440-331-1234
Work: 440-987-6543

Date
(Space down 4 lines here and for the signature. If you're desperate to fit it all on one page, cut a line here. But, be consistent and also cut a line from the signature area.)
Jane Doe, Director
Human Resources
ABC Agency
Street
City, State Zip code

Dear Director Doe:

I am applying for ABC Agency's Corrections Officer II position. Deputy Director William Nash is familiar with my abilities and experience as a Corrections Officer II; but, I have enclosed my resume for your convenience.

While my experience and skills are summarized in the application and resume, you may be interested in several additional qualifications I will bring to this position:
*   Proven record as a Corrections Officer II;
*   5 years of practical experience in the culturally diverse, corrections field ranging from Corrections Officer I to Corrections Officer II; *(Years strengthen expertise)*
*   Demonstrated ability to supervise employees and volunteers in a community-based, mentoring program; *(Link or elaborate on skills which may have been lost in the resume but are applicable to the field.)*
*   Ability to display initiative, enthusiasm and professionalism when working alone or as an integral member of a team. *(Use industry-specific terms in the closure.)*

I look forward to having the opportunity to discuss with you at greater length how I can become a contributing member of your corrections team. Thank you for your consideration.

Sincerely,

(Remember: since we cut 1 line after the date, we had to cut 1 line here.)
John Q. Smith

Enc *(Tells the reader of the letter there are enclosures i.e. the resume.)*

CONCLUSION

For resumes to resonate, they should parallel the employer's needs, highlight employee traits and be logical in format and function. Getting all the employment history organized into one, succinct resume page applicable to the criminal justice field is not easy, however: it's a painstaking, comprehensive process involving minute procedures and strategic decisions. But, if a draft is carefully designed, analyzed and crafted, the qualifications highlighted in the final resume will definitely resonate with the employer's qualifications! Consequently, you are ready for the next step: Chapter 12's Interesting Interviews!

SUGGESTED READING

Directory of Associations. (n.d.). http://www.marketingsource.com/associations

REFERENCES

Rue, L. W. & Byars, L. L. (1996). *Supervision: Key Link to Productivity.* Chicago, IL: Irwin of Time Mirror Higher Education Group, Inc.

McCoy, Chief W. I. (2001). Written Examination. In *The complete guide to hiring law enforcement officers: Based on a research study of the entry-level assessment center method* (pp. 63-86). Columbus, Ohio: Law Enforcement Foundation, Inc.

Oliver, Chief P. (2001). Selection Criteria for Law Enforcement Officers. In *The complete guide to hiring law enforcement officers: Based on a research study of the entry-level assessment center method* (pp. 49-62). Columbus, Ohio: Law Enforcement Foundation, Inc.

CHAPTER 12

INTERESTING INTERVIEWS

I don't care how much a man talks, if he only says it in a few words. -Josh Billings

AFTER READING THIS CHAPTER, YOU SHOULD KNOW
⇨ The typical types of interviews.
⇨ How to survive an assessment center abyss.
⇨ Whether "talking" is the same as "communicating".
⇨ What is involved in the communication process.
⇨ How to prepare for an interview.
⇨ What are 10 typical interview questions.
⇨ The 3 steps to a strong interview closure.
⇨ What a post-interview follow-up entails.

INTRODUCTION

After all the work you've been through, the interview process can be deceptively simple. Be forewarned, it is **not** simple: it's the critical last step to the job of your hopes and dreams. Therefore, it deserves time, planning, effort and preparation. Remember the criminal justice maxim: "Prior planning prevents poor performance!"

TYPICAL TYPES OF INTERVIEWS

There are two types of interviews: oral and assessment center. The **oral interview** is easier and more cost-effective for the employer and, thus, more frequently used. You're asked questions and you answer them with forthright logic and clarity. Seems simple! But, "seems" is the operative word. As explained in the rest of this chapter, considerable thought and effort should **still** be expended in preparing answers for the oral interview!

Conversely, "an assessment center is a standardized testing process that evaluates the ability of a candidate to perform specific job-related skills and behaviors...uses exercises and scenarios that simulate the target job...(and) predicts successful job performance (Oliver, 2001, p. 165)." Basically, the department designs exercises which are job-related, parallel "real-life" situations and do not require prior law enforcement knowledge.

SURVIVING THE ASSESSMENT CENTER ABYSS

While an abyss suggests an insurmountable chasm or trap, remember the assessment center is designed for someone who does **not** have prior knowledge and experience. Consequently, the process is comprehensive, **not** insurmountable, especially if you know the criterion to be assessed. McTaggart & Flannery (2001, p. 44) recommend a post-assessment (center) performance evaluation which includes--but is not be limited to--the ability to demonstrate "high moral and ethical standards...flexibility regarding direction given by management (and)...planning and preparation". They also suggest having the entry-level candidate demonstrate the ability to "...diffuse situations...gather information...interact effectively with people (and) ...maintain self-control."

To better prepare for an assessment center:

☑ **Review books and articles on *criminal justice* assessment centers.** Since assessment evaluates the candidate's fitness for a certain job, the exercises will be specific to that job and only that job. Thus, information on a business-based assessment center would have less applicability to the criminal justice field.

☑ **Analyze college textbooks on either law enforcement or corrections management.** In particular, read the chapters on hiring and skills assessment. Do you possess the desired skills? Have you reviewed and/or discussed the scenarios with a fellow criminal justice friend, associate or mentor? How would you respond?

☑ **Research college textbooks on human relations and ethics in criminal justice.** Use the "expert" opinions and critical thinking procedures as a guide. But, don't blindly duplicate the expert's suggestions or you're pretending to be someone you're not. Being hired on a pretense would mean you'd have to continue the pretense for the rest of your criminal justice career, just to fit in. How likely are you to stay...and be a happy, effective, productive employee...if you feel like a fraud?

THE COMMUNICATION PROCESS

Isn't "communicating" just the same as "talking? No, "talking" is not necessarily the same as "communicating". **Talking** can be someone speaking, without someone else, listening. You could be practicing a speech, talking to yourself, delirious, suffering from a disorder or just psychotic. On the other hand, "**communication** is a process involving several steps, among two or more persons, for the primary purpose of exchanging information" (Wallace, Roberson, & Steckler, 1997, p. 14). Therefore, effective communication only occurs when the exchange of information is made meaningful to the parties involved.

The communication process, then, also involves feedback between the person speaking (the sender) and the person responding (receiver). Feedback is the "process that allows persons transmitting information to correct and adjust messages to adapt to the receiver" (Wallace et al, 1997, p. 46). Feedback, then, indicates both people are listening and actively engaged in the exchange of information.

Confused? Consider any scenario where you have lost interest in the conversation. You could be on a too-long of telephone conversation, trying to watch television while someone is trying to talk with you or just bored. Do you remember the conversation? Can you act on the information imparted to you by the sender if you weren't receiving nor listening?

Feedback can be **verbal**: speaking the appropriate response to a question, adding your "two-cents worth", grunting "uh-huh" or just saying, "Yes, I agree" at the right moment. Conversely, feedback can also be **non-verbal**: failing to verbally respond at the appropriate moment in the conversation, looking confused or disbelieving, sneering or snoring. All denote a lack of receiving or feedback…without ever having said a word!

So, why the discourse on the communication process? Because, as Miller & Hess (2002, p. 152) cite, 55 percent of all communication is nonverbal; 38 percent is tone (pitch and inflection) and only 7 percent is the actual message. As a result, it's not enough to practice the verbal answers to possible interview questions. Unless the prospective employer is conducting the interview on-line, you must also practice your tone of voice and attend to the nonverbal cues you're emitting.

 **SPECIFYING SPATIAL RELATIONSHIPS**

There are two primary sources of non-verbal communication: spatial relationships and kinesics (body language). **Spatial** relationship denotes the distance or space between the sender and receiver. This distance can be **public** space, as defined by a public setting i.e. the physical structure of the interview room and furniture placement.

Conversely, a spatial relationship can be based on **personal** space: the distance you keep between yourself and others as a "personal safety zone". From the beginning of a criminal justice career, you're taught to maintain a speaking distance or "safety zone" of an "arm's length"; thus, an aggressive person has to overcome the distance of **two** arm's length to hurt you: yours and theirs. As a result, criminal justice practitioners are innately more comfortable if there is roughly an "arm's length"-distance between any two people.

How would YOU react to the following public, spatial dilemmas? (See answers on next page.)

☹ **#1: Removal of all manner of seating.** The removal of all chairs was a favorite ploy of the late-Director of the FBI, J. Edgar Hoover. What would you do?

_____

☹ **#2: Witness stand-style seating.** The interviewers sit on the long side of the table and one chair's placed parallel to the short side of the table. What do you do?

_____

☹ **#3: Open-seating.** There are chairs all around the table and the interviewers are standing. What do you do?

_____

☹ **#4: Multiple-seating.** Across from the interviewer, there are three chairs. Which chair do you choose and why?

_____

How did you do? Recommended answers to Spatial Relationship Quiz:

☺ **#1:** Pick up any chair in the room and place it directly in front of the interviewer. If there isn't a chair, stand as comfortably as possible (preferably with your arms at your side), directly in front of the interviewer.

☺ **#2:** Turn the chair toward the interviewers.

☺ **#3:** Keep standing. Try and be charming and friendly, yet professional. Wait until the interviewers sit down. Then, you sit directly in front of the interviewers.

☺ **#4:** Choose "formal" seating: the chair directly in front of the interviewer. Informal" seating would be the chair diagonally across from the interviewer. "Intimate" seating is directly next to the interviewer.

 **BASIC BODY LANGUAGE**

Body language or **kinesics** is the other primary source of nonverbal communication. "The first few moments of a personal contact are critical to the impression you make on others…(and) is called the **primacy effect**" (Miller & Hess, 2002, p. 158). Criminal justice practitioners must build on this primacy effect and, for their own safety and professional expertise, immediately and habitually analyze, assess and label a person's body language as: aggressive or non-aggressive; cooperative or uncooperative; comfortable or nervous; open and honest or deceptive/lying; confident or possessing a poor self-image. It's unrealistic to believe the criminal justice practitioner will relinquish this life-saving habit of labeling body language, just because he or she is conducting an interview.

Be cognizant of the messages your body language evokes. (The following applies to both male and female candidates):

☑ **Check your posture:** sit and walk "tall", shoulders back but be relaxed.

☎ **Call attention to your professionalism:** wear a suit, shine your shoes.

☺ **Be well-groomed:** get a haircut, keep your nails short and clean.

☹ **Limit your jewelry.** We're a traditional and safety-conscious field. Men shouldn't

150.

wear earrings, at least until after they're hired and only then if allowed. Women should wear ½ inch or smaller posts (no clips, hoops nor lever-backs), to prevent earlobe damage by a bad person. A watch and ring are allowed.1

☞ **Give a handshake to all interviewers (whether male or female), at beginning and end of interview.** Don't appear to be biased nor disrespectful to the interviewers.

◎ **Target the speaker.** Answer and make eye contact with the interviewer who asks the question, first; but, be sure to make eye contact with the other interviewers during the rest of your answer.

💣 **Avoid unnecessary gestures,** i.e. fidgeting, shrugs, changing positions, etc....

★ **Practice, practice, practice!** Practice in front of a mirror, friends, a video-camera. Notice and practice deleting annoying gestures, insincere and insecure body language.

 TEMPERING YOUR TONE

Now that you've addressed 55 percent of your communication process (nonverbal), let's discuss the 38 percent: your tone. **Answer the following questions concerning your tone of voice in an interview. (See the answers on the next page):**

AGREE   DISAGREE

1. Effective communication is a skill.
2. Criminal justice employees need to be effective communicators.
3. You can show contempt by your tone of voice.
4. You can intimate condescension with voice inflection.
5. A monotone voice is an effective communication style.
6. A person can speak and listen at the same time.
7. A person should show excitement by speaking quickly.
8   Confidence and self-control are reflected in a tone of voice.
9. Sarcasm can be used in an interview, if it's necessary to make a point or answer a question.
10. An appropriate tone can be an advantage in the communication process.

How did you do? Answers to Tempering Your Tone Quiz:

1. **Agree**, effective communication skills can be learned or improved.

2. **Agree**, not only can a criminal justice employee take command of a situation by the tone of voice, but that same employee can lose control if the tone is inappropriate or utilizes one which could evoke contempt.

3. **Absolutely agree**. Practice on a good friend if you're not sure whether this is true.

4. **Agree**, condescension can positively drip from each word spoken.

5. **Disagree**, a monotone voice is boring. Consequently, it's difficult to sustain interest in the speaker and his/her message over any length of time.

6. **Disagree**. There's science behind the saying, "That's why you were given 2 ears and one mouth, so you could listen twice as much as you speak!" It's physically impossible to speak and listen at the same time.

7. **Disagree**. Speaking quickly can result in garbled speech and poor pronunciation. If you're excited, smile as you're speaking or lean forward in your seat.

8. **Agree**. Haven't you ever heard someone say, "S/he sounded confident!"

9. **Disagree**, sarcasm is never appropriate in an interview: it's demeaning to the receiver and the sender.

10. **Agree**, or why have we been discussing this issue for so long?

 VIGOROUS VERBAL RESPONSES

Being vigorous does not mean yelling at each other: it means being definitive in your beliefs, thoughtful and logical in your responses. You've already addressed the primacy effect. Now you must overcome the **"four-minute barrier**...the point in an initial meeting at which most people have formed a positive or negative opinion about the individual with whom they are communicating" (Miller & Hess, 2002, p. 159).

With less than 4 minutes to enhance your communication and establish your supremacy as the preferred candidate, can you afford to overlook even a 7 percent advantage?

Review the chart on the next page for communication enhancers:

COMMUNICATION ENHANCER	HOW TO DEMONSTRATE
1. COURTESY	+Greet the interviewers with, "Good morning" or "Good afternoon". +Shake hands with **all** interviewers. +Address interviewers by rank, title or at least, sir or ma'am. +At the end, thank the interviewers for their time and shake their hands again.
2. ESPRIT DE CORPS/TEAM-PLAYER	+Include "we" & "team" in your answer. +Ask how the shift/department usually responds in this type of situation. +Praise co-workers and supervisors, leave the blame, anger and discontent at home. +Answer in a long-term context, "In 5 years, I expect to be here, hopefully promoted to…."
3. AVOID PROFANITY/ANGER	+Do we really need to explain this one?
4. BE POSITIVE	+Be as sincere, honest and open to discussion and new ideas as possible. +Wait until the entire question is asked before trying to answer it!
5. ACTIVE LISTENING	+Give verbal and non-verbal feedback to show interest and attentiveness. +Listen carefully for help from leading questions. EX: "When performing community policing duties…." The "community policing" cue intimates your answer should include comments about problem-solving, respect and the community-agency team.
6. USE APPROPRIATE SEMANTICS	+Use buzz phrases and words appropriate to the position and field. +Do not use jargon--unless you use it appropriately, in the proper context.
7. AVOID STEREOTYPES & GENERALIZATIONS	+Avoid biased and judgmental phrases and words like, "Those people…." +All generalization are bad!

PREPARING FOR AN INTERVIEW

PRIOR PLANNING PREVENTS POOR (Interview) PERFORMANCE!
PRIOR to the interview, research the organization:

★ **Local newspaper.** Within the last year, are there any articles on the department in the local newspaper? Are the articles predominantly supportive or critical? Does this information impact the image you have of the organization?

★ **Agency website.** Does the organization have a website? Does it foster a positive or negative image? Does the information impact the image you have of the organization?

★ **Incorporation.** If appropriate, take credit for your research and planning skills by incorporating the **positive** results of your research into your interview. **Law enforcement example:** "According to your website (or name the local newspaper), you've reduced violent crime by 25 percent. What are your plans to maintain that reduction?" **Corrections example:** "According to your website (or newspaper), you're accepting federal inmates now. How does that impact your officer-to-inmate ratio? Do you plan to hire more officers in the near future?"

PLANNING *how* to answer the questions is critical:

★ **Illegal questions.** Interviewers **should** be trained on hiring legalities, as previously discussed in Chapter 10. But, how will you respond if asked an illegal question?
Choice #1: "You can't ask that!"
Choice #2 (With sarcasm): "How does that question relate to this job?"
Choice #3 (With<u>out</u> sarcasm): "How does that question relate to this job?"
Choice #4: If you can tolerate the question being asked, answer it politely, succinctly, Professionally and with as little negative body language as possible.
Our Choice: #3 or #4, depending on the question and your desire for the job.

★ **Immoral questions.** Your choices (and ours) are the same.

PREVENT mistakes by being prepared. Interpersonal communications have 3 steps: opening, body/discussion and closure. What image do you want to project at each step?

POOR attitude and appearance should be left at home. Remember your success as a communicator is 55 percent body language (appearance) and 38 percent tone (attitude).

PERFORMANCE should be practiced, diligently and often. Ask a supportive friend or relative to critique your performance from a professional perspective. How do you look? Did you utilize your "communications enhancers" from the previous page?

TEN TYPICAL INTERVIEW QUESTIONS

1. **WHAT CAN YOU TELL ME ABOUT YOURSELF?**
   HINT: Have you heard the joke, "How do you eat an elephant? One bite at a time!" This question is an "elephant" ![elephant] ! It's too big to eat at once! Take care of it easily: slowly break it into little pieces you **can** address.
   GOOD: "What would you like to know?"
   BETTER: "What would you like to know…about my educational background or work history?"
   YOUR ANSWER:_____

   _____

2. **WHAT IS YOUR GREATEST WEAKNESS?**
   HINT: The employer is hoping you'll try so hard to be truthful, you'll be too candid. Answer instead with a carefully chosen, truthful but harmless weakness.
   GOOD: "I know my spelling could be better."
   BETTER: "I know my spelling could be better. So, I carry a dictionary in my briefcase…just in case I need to double-check the spelling on a report."
   YOUR ANSWER:_____

   _____

3. **WHAT IS YOUR GREATEST ACCOMPLISHMENT?**
   HINT: What a conundrum! If you answer, you're bragging and have lost credibility. If you don't answer, you sound unprepared. First, choose a job related accomplishment. Second, if possible, choose a team project. Third, make sure it's measurable and documented…otherwise, you're bragging **and** exaggerating!
   GOOD: "On my last job, I reduced inventory shrinkage (theft) by 8 percent."
   BETTER: "On my last job, I assisted my department in reducing inventory shrinkage by 8 percent."
   YOUR ANSWER:_____

   _____

   _____

4. **WHAT ARE YOUR SHORT-TERM GOALS? (Think 5 years or less.)**
HINT: This is an objective and should be specific, measurable and realistic.
GOOD: "I intend to finish my college degree."
BETTER: "I intend to finish my college degree, so I can assist this organization in supporting its mission and meeting its goals."
YOUR ANSWER:_____

_____

5. **WHAT PERSONAL CHARACTERISTICS DO YOU BELIEVE ARE NECESSARY FOR SUCCESS IN THIS POSITION?**

HINT: Another ! You **are** allowed to ask questions i.e., "Could you clarify that question with an example?" At least you appear thoughtful and have gained a little insight into what answer the employer is seeking.
GOOD: "I believe, to be successful in this position, a person should be honest, dedicated, diligent, a good communicator and be service-oriented."
BETTER: "I believe, to be successful in this position, a person should be honest, dedicated to the organization's goals and standards, diligent at work, have effective communication skills and be service-oriented."
YOUR ANSWER:_____

_____

6. **HOW WELL DO YOU WORK UNDER PRESSURE? CAN YOU GIVE ME A FEW EXAMPLES?**
HINT: First, recognize stress is a dangerous and constant threat in the criminal justice field. Second, you do **not** have to give examples and are less likely to make a mistake if you keep your answer to **one particular** example.
GOOD: "One particular example of my working under pressure stands out. We were short a staff member, but had to complete a project by the end of the work day: our director was presenting it the next morning. So, we worked late and completed the project under deadline."
BETTER: "One particular example of my working under pressure stands out. We were short a staff member. But, as project coordinator, it was my job to ensure the city council project was completed by the end of the work day: our director was presenting to the council the next morning. So, we all worked late and completed the project as soon as possible. I hand-delivered the completed project directly to the director's residence and offered to be available an hour before the presentation, in case the director had any questions or changes."
YOUR ANSWER:_____

_____

7. **DESCRIBE A FEW PROBLEMS YOU HAD AT WORK AND HOW YOU HANDLED THEM.**

HINT: Narrow the field to **one** harmless conflict that included a win-win solution.

GOOD: "I remember one particular problem I had with a co-worker. We worked different shifts but shared an office. We had problems because he'd leave the office messy and I'm neat and organized. So, one day, I couldn't take the mess any more: we talked out our problems and came to an understanding."

BETTER: "I remember one particular problem I had with a co-worker. We worked different shifts but shared an office. He seldom filed his paperwork, so I had difficulty in finding documents. So, I made an appointment to meet him and we talked over the situation. We eventually decided on a compromise: he would place all his unfiled documents in the "in-box" I'd put on the top of the file cabinet. He'd file one week and I'd file the next. Then, after 1 month, we'd review the compromise and see if we needed to make any changes to the solution."

YOUR ANSWER:

8. **WHAT CAN YOU TELL ME ABOUT YOUR PAST SUPERVISORS?**

HINT: What an and a potential conflict! After all, you are answering a question **about** a supervisor **to** a supervisor!

GOOD: "What would you like to know?"

BETTER: "I believe my past supervisors would speak well of my accomplishments and work as a team player. After all, as you can see in my application, they have agreed to be references for this job opening with your organization."

YOUR ANSWER:

9. **WHY DO YOU WANT TO WORK FOR THIS ORGANIZATION?**

HINT: "Sell" your planning and research skills by re-iterating highlights of your research results. (Remember the previous **5 P's** discussion?)

GOOD: "Based on what I read in your website/local newspaper, I believe we have things in common and I can be a productive member of your organization."

BETTER: "Based on what I read in your website/newspaper, we share similar goals and values, such as (list a few details here). Consequently, I believe I would be a productive team player with your organization."

YOUR ANSWER:

10. WHY SHOULD I HIRE YOU OVER THE NEXT APPLICANT?
HINT: Highlight key qualifications discussed in the interview. Be careful not to brag nor be condescending toward the other applicants.
GOOD: "As we discussed, I am qualified for this position, and am a team-player. I will work hard to be an effective employee with your organization."
BETTER: "As we discussed, I am qualified for this position because I can (list key qualifications **the employer** mentioned but **you** possess). Finally, I will work hard to be a team player and an effective employee for your organization."
YOUR ANSWER: _____

_____

3 STEPS TO A STRONG INTERVIEW CLOSURE!

1. ANSWERING THE INTERVIEWER'S LAST QUESTION: "DO YOU HAVE ANY QUESTIONS?"
HINT: Do **not** ask about salary or benefits: wait until the final interview or conditional offer of employment to decide if the salary and benefits are acceptable. Do **not** ask, "When will I hear from you?" **They** are doing the hiring, so **they** set (or ignore) the schedule. Remember: this **is** your last chance to shine!
GOOD: "No, thank you. You've addressed all the questions I have at this time."
BETTER: "Yes. What plans do **you** have for the organization in the next 2 years?" This question is fool-proof. You don't have to remember anything and they have to answer the question.
YOUR ANSWER: _____

_____

2. STATE DEFINITIVELY YOU WANT THE JOB! Practice saying, "Thank you for the opportunity to be interviewed. I'm really looking forward to working for your organization." The hiring process is too lengthy, time-consuming and expensive to risk having to repeat simply because the employer is unsure of your answer. If **you** are unsure of your answer, still say you're interested: you are still a candidate and have gained time to decide whether to accept the job, if offered.

3. MIND YOUR MANNERS! Thank each interviewer by his/her full name and rank, i.e. "Thank you for your time, Capt. Smith." Finally, be sure to give a firm (but not crushing) handshake to each and every interviewer.

POST-INTERVIEW FOLLOW-UP

It's within 24 hours of the interview, have you done the following?

☑ **Assess.** Discuss your interview with a supportive friend or relative. How did you do? On what questions did you excel? Which questions were difficult? Could you improve on your body language, tone/delivery and/or answers for the next interview?

☑ **De-stress.** Now that you've assessed your performance, de-stress. Read a book, work out, go for a walk, enjoy your favorite past-time, go out to dinner or a movie with a friend or relative. Just be careful. There is a fine line between celebrating and overindulging and the latter could not only erode your professional image but your non-criminal record.

☑ **Written a thank you letter.** The letter should be sent to the highest ranking interviewer and similar in style to your résumé's cover letter.
   + **First paragraph:** thank the interviewers (preferably, by full name and title) for granting an interview on whatever date the interview occurred.
   + **Second paragraph:** highlight qualifications discussed as a result of the questions asked in the interview. Indicate the memorable statements or qualifications you believe most impressed the interviewers.
   + **Last paragraph:** again thank the interviewers for their consideration and stress how interested you are in working for the organization.

☑ **Prepare your schedule for a second interview.** Do not dwell on the fact that a second interview will probably occur, but do the following:
   + **Determine your availability over the next 2-3 weeks:** plan on a full day; but, hope for a half-day.
   + **Practice your interview answers.** To determine the truthfulness and accuracy of your answers, you may be asked the same questions. Be prepared to more fully discuss your career and life goals, interview questions, accomplishments, personal history and work-related scenarios. An assessment center could be scheduled.
   + **Practice your meal manners.** Many employers want to observe the candidate in a more social and public setting. Simple behaviors such as using salt and/or pepper on the food before tasting the meal has worked against the candidate: employers may conclude the candidate makes hasty judgments based on appearance, rather than evaluating the facts.

☑ **Expect to be interviewed by the ultimate decision-makers.** If possible, contact the organization for the correct spelling and pronunciation of the executive director, human resource director and finance officer.

☑ **Offer of employment.** The employment offer could occur with or without a second interview. The employer determines when the decision will occur and, the offer made.

CONCLUSION

In this chapter, we've discussed the preparation and procedures involved in the comprehensive and stressful interview stage of the hiring process. Since an oral interview begins with the meaningful exchange of information, the communication process was foundation of this chapter. Each element of the communication process was examined, from kinesics (body language), delivery (tone) to the actual message (exchange of information). Whether the organization utilized an assessment center or a more traditional oral interview, this chapter's re-occurring theme has been the necessity of planning and practice. Plan the image you wish to convey and the initial contact with the interviewers. Practice the answers to the ten typical interview questions. Plan and practice for the follow-up interview. Above all, remember the interview stage is generally the last chance you have to definitively state why the employer should hire **you**…and not someone else!

REFERENCES

Miller, L. & Hess, K. (2002). *The police in the community: Strategies for the 21st century.* Belmont, CA: Wadsworth/Thomson Learning.

Oliver, Chief P. 2001. The Entry Level Assessment Center. In *The complete guide to hiring law enforcement officers: Based on a research study of the entry-level assessment center method* (pp. 164-176). Columbus, OH: Law Enforcement Foundation, Inc.

Wallace, H., Roberson, C., & Steckler, C. (1997). *Written and interpersonal communication methods for law enforcement.* Upper Saddle River, NJ: Prentice Hall.

CHAPTER 13

IN LAW ENFORCEMENT, WHAT HAPPENS AFTER...?

"The only way to discover the limits of the possible is to go beyond them into the impossible" -Arthur C. Clarke

AFTER READING THIS CHAPTER, YOU SHOULD KNOW
⇨ "Standard" changes which occur as a result of a new career.
⇨ The 4 stages of career development and their impact on your career.
⇨ The difference between probation and in-service (field) training.
⇨ What attitudes and behaviors exemplify the "police subculture".
⇨ How to compare and contrast career expectations versus career realities.
⇨ The results of the final self-assessment in your career plan.

INTRODUCTION

Congratulations! You've succeeded in evaluating your preferences, skills, knowledge, values and general career interests. You know what *you* want and need in an employer and how to find an employer who can effectively match or exceed *your general* career-related needs. Furthermore, after reading Chapters 3 and 4, you should have narrowed *your specific* career interests to either private or public law enforcement and, if you chose the latter, which level of employment *you* would prefer (municipal, county, regional, state or federal). You've also worked through the process of planning *your* career, preparing for pre-employment stages of testing and interviewing...all while developing an effective resume which highlights *your* qualifications.

But, have you really thought about what a new career means? What stages exist in career development? What's the difference between a probationary period and in-service or field training? What exactly is the police subculture and what does it have to do with you and your career, especially if you're interested in the private sector? Is there a difference between your career expectations and your career realities? Lastly, what are the results of your final self-assessment? Do you need to re-visit your career plan and goals?

"STANDARD" CHANGES IN YOUR NEW CAREER

Whether interested in private or public sector employment, are you ready for the following changes?

CHANGE	READY	MAY BE READY	NOT READY	IF NOT READY, WHAT NOW?
1. NEW IDENTITY with your new career.				
2. NEW WORK COLLEAGUES				
3. NEW AGENCY CULTURE (See section on "Police Subculture")				
4. ROTATING SHIFT SCHEDULE				
5. BEING "ON-DUTY" 24/7 (Expected to respond 24 hours a day, 7 days a week)				
6. NEW SCHEDULE AT HOME (because of rotating shifts)				
7. LOSS OF OLD FRIENDS (See also "Police Subculture")				
8. DEFENDER OF JUSTICE SYSTEM (re item seen in media)				

(Adapted from McClelland, 2001, p. 307).

STAGES OF CAREER DEVELOPMENT

You're starting a new chapter in your life and the *4 stages of career development* apply whether you're interested in private or public law enforcement:

1) **TRANSITION:** From the first day, through the in-service training process (about the first 3 months for public sector, varies for private), you're wondering whether you've made the right decision or should return to your old career and lifestyle.

   ☞ **Characterized** by youthful enthusiasm, energy, ambition, education/training in topics and techniques.

   ☀ **Changes in lifestyle** occur regarding family and friends who don't want to deal with your rotating schedule, re-assessing of marital effort (who does what, when?) and new financial obligations (cost of training, moving to residence-city, new work clothes/suits/uniforms, equipment, mileage, etc....)

   ◎ **Starting in-service training:** The public sector calls this time FTO because of the Field Training Officer who oversees the training; private sector either calls the person a training officer or mentor. In both cases, it's the training officer's responsibility to socialize you into the new organizational culture: ensure you understand the informal language, formal procedures and processes, and preferred attitudes and behaviors of the new career. The training officer *should* be supportive and assist you in making the transition from old career to your new one. Unfortunately, sometimes the training officer is simply chosen for scheduling or seniority-reasons, rather than for interest *and skill* in helping you succeed.

   ☯ **Changes in attitude and language:** starting to adopt the new organizational culture, resulting in a barrier between you and your friends from your "old life".

   ☯ *Your* **chance to decide it** *you* **like it here, in your new organization.**

2) **PROBATION:** Usually the first year (both private and public sector) and includes the training officer period. Did you choose the right career--and right organization?

   ☯ **Changes in attitude continue.** But, careful about which attitude you develop! Be wary of the jaded veteran who tells you to "forget everything you learned in the academy or college: I'll show you the *right* way." Would you want to be operated on by a doctor who discarded everything learned in medical school?

☯ **Changes in language and increasing use of authoritative** (dictatorial?) **tone could continue to build barriers between you and loved ones.** Hopefully, you are still working to keep healthy relationships with non-law enforcement friends and loved ones as a primary focus of your life.

☯ **Changes in behavior starting.** You're making minor mistakes and starting to develop organizational culture (police subculture?) habits. Personal excess such as substance abuse or drinking after shift may occur. Try to diminish the effects of these negative behaviors by embracing this probationary period as a valuable professional process and opportunity for occupational growth and advancement.

☯ **Corrective instruction** is the training officer's way of assisting you in making the transition and should not be viewed as personal or embarrassing.

💣 **"Serve at will":** under statutory and/or administrative probation, you "serve at will". In other words, you can be dismissed or fired for no cause--even from employment in the public sector.

3) **MIDDLE STAGE:** You know what to do, think and feel. You can be trusted and work according to the organizational culture or police subculture. You have either primarily experienced personal and professional advancement, or problems and obstacles. You've tried to be loyal to associates, without exhibiting blind allegiance; exercised your authority, without becoming rude or dictatorial; been aware of dangerous situations, without becoming socially isolated from citizens; above all, tried to balance the demands of the hours and job with those of maintaining a healthy personal and family life. Conversely, growing discontentment may be mounting and resulting in exhibitions of unprofessional or undesirable conduct. Which do *you* think you'll be experiencing? Are you prepared for either? Do you have the dedication to follow your career through to the end?

☯ **Changes in behavior, attitude and jargon continue:** corrupting influences of too much authority (legal right to act) and power (personal ability to act) could result in opportunities for infidelity and/or substance abuse. Have you kept non-law enforcement-related friends and activities?

💣 **"(Public) (l)aw enforcement officers are 300 percent more likely to suffer from alcoholism than the average American"** (Gaines, L. K., Kaune, M., & Miller, R. L., 2001, p. 178).

💣 **"The stress of police work may help explain why ten times as many cops die by their own hands...as are killed in the line of duty (*New York Times*, January 1, 1997, p. 12)"** (Cole, G. F., & Smith, C. E., 1999, p. 129). For both private- and public-sectors, organizational stress from irregular shifts and hours, operational stress from working with less-than-desirable individuals and personal stress, resulting from both, may start to take their toll. Can you have a positive

164.

attitude to balance the negativity in your professional life? Again, have you made an effort to maintain a healthy, mentally, socially, and physically active personal life outside of work?

☑ **Combat stressors and stereotypes by being professional on- and off-duty!**

4) **LATER STAGE:** Nearing the end of your *professional* life, you may or may not have seen your last promotion take place. Behavioral, attitudinal and lifestyle changes are probably permanent. Good health may persist, but you react at a slower pace. Now, what do you do, continue to dispense professional service? Adopt the regrettable and negative "short-timers" attitude and "do a straight 8"? (Work eight hours, with a minimal amount of effort, and go home.) Find a life, after your professional law enforcement life? **Above all, have you *planned* (financially, psychologically, and behaviorally) for a post-career life?**

THE POLICE SUBCULTURE

Stop thinking about law enforcement as glamorous and exciting. As the anonymous police adage goes, "Police work is 99 percent boredom and 1% sheer terror." "A **subculture** is made up of the symbols, beliefs, values, and attitudes shared by members of a subgroup within the society" (Cole, G. F., & Smith, C. E., 1999, p. 126). In other words, the subculture will help you define police work and your related work roles. **Are you ready for the impact of the 3 elements of the police subculture on your life?**

SUBCULTURE ELEMENT	READY?	IF NOT READY, WHAT NOW?
1. THREAT OF DANGER (Hostility, feelings of being under constant attack, suspicion and caution, on-duty 24 hours a day.)		
2. AUTHORITY (Exercise appropriate use of force?)		
3. ISOLATION (Cynicism, stresses of shift work, Us vs. Them/ the public.)		

(Adapted from Cole, G. F., & Smith, C. E., 1999, pp. 127-130).

CAREER EXPECTATIONS VS. CAREER REALITIES

We'd be the first to wish you luck in finding your dream job and a career which meets-- even exceeds--your expectations. But, we'd be remiss if we didn't try and prevent you from experiencing stress, frustration, disillusionment or even pain because your career expectations weren't realistic.

Consequently, whether you're interested in private- or public-sector law enforcement, carefully consider the following questions as a means to gently and pro-actively evaluate your enthusiastic expectations against a more-tempered reality. In other words, **answer the following true/false questions:**

_____   1.   I expect to be accepted as an equal by my peers.

_____   2.   I expect to have a supportive in-service training officer.

_____   3.   My college experience can only help me in this field.

_____   4.   Because of the police subculture, we will all be united by common philosophies, goals and objectives.

_____   5.   I'm looking forward to an exciting, fast-paced career.

_____   6.   With my skills, knowledge and abilities, I don't anticipate any problem in being promoted.

_____   7.   Since diversity is so widely accepted, prejudice has been virtually eliminated.

_____   8.   Now that I know what constitutes the police subculture, I don't anticipate any problem in being able to combat its potentially negative effects.

_____   9.   Because you would be a "big fish in a little pond", a smaller department would afford greater promotional opportunities.

_____   10.   I know where I will work and expect to be there until retirement.

How did you do on the "Career Expectations vs. Career Realities" quiz?

Answer--Short Version: The more "true" answers you have, the more enthusiastically optimistic you are and, perhaps, unrealistic in your career expectations.

Answers--Long Version: ALL ANSWERS ARE FALSE! Read on for details:

1.   **I expect to be accepted as an equal by my peers.** It's an inevitable result of human interaction that someone, somewhere will not accept you as an "equal".

2.   **I expect to have a supportive in-service training officer.** As previously noted, the training officer is not always the best qualified. Furthermore, there's a lot of stress, paperwork and liability (negligent training civil suits) attached to the training officer position. Not everyone is willing to do the job.

3.   **My college experience can only help me in this field.** Professionally, yes, college will help you. Personally, "old school" officers who didn't have college, but worked their way up the career ladder may be against a "college kid". **Just because you're breathing, you may accidentally represent:**
    (a) **mortality** i.e. you're the "new" kid, so the veteran must be "old".
    (b) **change** i.e. "If that idea would work, we would have done it a long time ago. If it ain't broke, don't fix it, kid!"
    (c) **a threat to status quo in the organization** i.e. "Who do you think you are to just come in here and tell me how things should be done?"
    (d) **a threat to status quo in the field** i.e. "There was a time when you didn't need a damn college degree, just brains and common sense…Things haven't changed all that much that you need college to do *this* job!"

4.   **Because of the police subculture, we will all be united by common philosophies, goals and objectives.** Not necessarily so. First, remember that isolation is an element of the police subculture: no one said it was relegated only to personal life *outside* the organization. Secondly, even if you chose the private-sector for your career interest, we contend the more para-military in structure, the more likely the police subculture will also infect the private law enforcement organization. Lastly, see the answers to Question #1-3.

5.   **I'm looking forward to an exciting, fast-paced career.** Wrong field. Remember the previously quoted adage about "99% boredom and 1% terror". "Reality t.v." is *not* reality! What, you never acted up in front of a camera?

6.   **With my skills, knowledge and abilities, I don't anticipate any problem in being promoted.** Neither do we…presuming there *are* promotional opportunities, the promotional position is actually funded, you pass the

necessary promotional criteria, there are no civil suits against the promotional procedure and the person with promoting authority agrees that you're the best person for the job. (Even in civil service testing, promotional procedures can say the successful candidate must be chosen from the top 3 candidates. They do not mandate *you* are the one promoted.) Maybe you're not so sure of being promoted and this procedure isn't as rosy a picture as you thought?

7. **Since diversity is so widely accepted, prejudice has been virtually eliminated.** *False. Discrimination*, illegal actions of prejudice, have been virtually eliminated by progressive organizations. But, we are all prejudiced: we all have stereotypes, preferences or conditions which exclude people from being accepted. But, do we, as private- and public-sector law enforcement professionals, do our best to reduce or eliminate the likelihood of that prejudice becoming an act of discrimination?

8. **Now that I know what constitutes the police subculture, I don't anticipate any problem in being able to combat its potentially negative effects.** While we do not have any statistics to back our statement (only over 50 years combined experience in the field), it's the contention of the authors that *all* public (and paramilitary-style, private) law enforcement organizations experience police subculture. The question is whether the subculture is the dominant or minority influence on law enforcement employee's behavior.

9. **Because you would be a "big fish in a little pond", a smaller department would afford greater promotional opportunities.** *False.* Smaller departments may afford greater opportunities for personal and professional growth and development because, by definition, everyone is a generalist and cross-trained. But, promotions can only exist if they are philosophically appropriate for the mission and structure of the organization, financially supported (staff *and* resources), and produce expected and effective results. Consequently, smaller departments are *less* likely to offer promotions. Why would the smaller agency need promotions? The officers already do their jobs without the additional link in the chain of command and at considerable savings in cost, competition, procedures and civil litigation (negligent hiring, retention, supervision and/or training) to the organization.

10. **I know where I will work and expect to be there until retirement.** Hopefully you're right. But, there are always unexpected circumstances: layoffs; agency re-organizations and consolidations; marriages and births requiring re-assessment of career plans; deaths of friends, partners and loved-ones; debilitating work-related injuries; family and personal obligations; changes in expectations or careers; and traumatic personal and professional experiences. Again, we wish you luck in finding your dream job and a career which meets--even exceeds--your expectations...and spares you any of the above epiphanies or life-altering situations.

FINAL SELF-ASSESSMENT

In Chapter 9, you designed a career plan to achieve your occupational choice. In this chapter, you re-evaluated your career expectations against the realities of the law enforcement field and, maybe, the police subculture. **Now, answer the following:**

1)   **What changes in your life can you expect?**

   a. Personal Changes:_____

   _____

   b. Financial Changes:_____

   _____

   c. Relationship Changes:_____

   _____

   d. Professional Changes:_____

   _____

   e. Lifestyle Changes:_____

   _____

2)   **Prioritize these changes, according to their importance to *your* career plan:**

   #1 Priority:_____

   #2 Priority:_____

   #3 Priority:_____

   #4 Priority:_____

   #5 Priority:_____

3) Assess the likelihood these priorities (changes) will occur:

PRIORITY/CHANGE	NOT LIKELY TO OCCUR	LIKELY TO OCCUR	VERY LIKELY
#1:			
#2:			
#3:			
#4:			
#5:			

4) Using the results from Question #3, re-assess your priority list:

#1 Priority:_____

#2 Priority:_____

#3 Priority:_____

#4 Priority:_____

#5 Priority:_____

5) Changes and priorities can only occur if a conscious choice and effort is made. Do you *want* to make these changes in priorities?

PRIORITY/CHANGE	DO YOU WANT TO DO THIS?	WHAT DO YOU DO NOW?
#1:		
#2:		
#3:		
#4:		
#5:		

CONCLUSION

Several final thoughts. A few law enforcement professionals we know succumbed to the temptations of the field: disenchanted attitudes; substance abuse; abusive behavior; suicide; disintegrated marriages; and/or illegal activities. Still fewer in number, succumbed to premature illnesses, debilitating and permanent injuries or even death incurred in the line of duty. Most of the law enforcement professionals we know went on to successful careers. They were successful not only from their levels of professional achievement, but also, personal growth and development. Those successful law enforcement practitioners put themselves before others; were considerate to and respectful of the public; made reasonable attempts to work closely, effectively and in support of peers; took their commitment to their careers and career fields, seriously. They are understandably proud of their accomplishments.

But, this text is about *you*: how will *you* do? After reading and working through this text, you are as prepared for your career field as possible. How does your Chapter 9 career plan balance against career expectations and career realities resulting from this chapter? Have you planned appropriately, made the commitment of time, effort, resources and longevity necessary to succeed in the field? Are you going to be one of the successful professionals or one of those who succumbed to the temptation of the organizational culture, police subculture and stressors of this field? *In your sincere and final assessment, do you have what it takes to make this field your career choice?*

SUGGESTED READING

ANY WEBSITE OR BOOK RELATING TO A HOBBY, SPORT, LEISURE ACTIVITIES WHICH CATCH YOUR INTEREST!

American Society of Association Executives (over 6,000 associations) at http://info.asaenet.org/gateway/OnlineAssocSlist.html

Directory of Associations (over 2,500 associations) at http://www.marketingsource.com/associations

Encyclopedia of Associations: check your local library for this book of over 23,000 national and international associations.

National Trade & Professional Associations Directory: check your local library for this book of "...about 7,600 trade associations, professional societies, labor unions, and technical organizations" (McClelland, 2001, p. 227).

REFERENCES

Cole, G. F., & Smith, C. E. (1999). *Criminal justice in america.* Belmont, CA: Wadsworth.

Gaines, L. K., Kaune, M., & Miller, R. L. (2001). *Criminal justice in action: The core.* Belmont, CA: Wadsworth.

McClelland, Carol. (2001). *Changing careers for dummies.* New York, NY: Hungry Minds, Inc.

CHAPTER 14

IN CORRECTIONS, WHAT HAPPENS AFTER…?

"If you do not feel yourself growing in your work and you life broadening and deepening, if your task is not a perpetual tonic to you, you have not found your place.
-Orson Sweet Marden

AFTER READING THIS CHAPTER, YOU SHOULD KNOW
⇨ "Standard" changes which occur as a result of a new career.
⇨ The 4 stages of career development and their impact on your career.
⇨ What attitudes and behaviors exemplify the "inmate subculture".
⇨ How to compare and contrast career expectations versus career realities.
⇨ The results of the final self-assessment in your career plan.

INTRODUCTION

At this point, we expect you to have chosen either this chapter for corrections-based information and insights or the law enforcement-based Chapter 13: "In Law Enforcement, What Happens After…? You may be one of those rare individuals who explore both chapters because you're practical (after all, they are part of the book you paid for and you want to get your money's worth) or intellectually curious (you're simply expanding your career outlook and opportunities). If so, then a special congratulations! You get to read similar introductions in both Chapters 13 *and* 14--or can skip directing to the next section.

In reaching this chapter, you've succeeded in evaluating your preferences, skills, knowledge, values and general career interests. You know what *you* want and need in an employer and how to find an employer who can effectively match or exceed *your general* career-related needs. Furthermore, after reading Chapters 6 and 7, you should have narrowed *your specific* career interests to either private or public corrections and, if you chose the latter, which level of employment *you* would prefer (municipal, county, state or federal). You've also worked through the process of planning *your* career, preparing for pre-employment stages of testing and interviewing…all while developing an effective resume which highlights *your* qualifications.

But, have you really thought about what a new career means? What stages exist in career development? What exactly is the inmate subculture and what does it have to do with you and your career? Is there a difference between your career expectations and your career realities? Lastly, what are the results of your final self-assessment? Do you need to re-visit your career plan and goals?

"STANDARD" CHANGES IN YOUR NEW CAREER

Whether interested in private or public sector employment, are you ready for the following changes?

CHANGE	READY	MAY BE READY	NOT READY	IF NOT READY, WHAT NOW?
1. NEW IDENTITY with your new career.				
2. NEW WORK COLLEAGUES				
3. NEW AGENCY CULTURE				
4. WORKING WITH INMATES				
5. IF C.O., BEING LOCKED UP				
6. ROTATING SHIFT SCHEDULE				
7. NEW SCHEDULE AT HOME				
8. LOSS OF OLD FRIENDS				
9. DEFENDING WHY NOT ALL "CONS" ARE LOCKED UP				

(Adapted from McClelland, 2001, p. 307

STAGES OF CAREER DEVELOPMENT

You're starting a new chapter in your life and the *4 stages of career development* apply whether you're interested in private or public corrections:

1) **TRANSITION:** It's you first day on the job as a corrections officer and you've just passed through your first checkpoint: the door slams shut behind and you hear a thud as the lock engages. Conversely, it's your first day on the job as a probation or parole officer, you're escorted to a sub-divided office, a few officers are on the phone, others are busily doing paperwork. You're handed a pile of folders, pointed to a desk and told, "Welcome Aboard, Rookie. Hope you last!" In either case, you're wondering whether you've made the right decision or should return to your old career lifestyle.

☞ **Characterized** by youthful enthusiasm, energy, ambition, education/training in topics and techniques.

💣 **Changes in lifestyle occur,** especially regarding family and friends who don't want to deal with your rotating schedule, re-assessing of marital effort and new financial obligations (cost of training, moving to residence-city, new work clothes, equipment, mileage, etc....)

☑ **Check the policies and procedures on everything.** Begin learning the policies, procedures, philosophies, command structure and organizational culture. Start to understand how to work with inmates/offenders and the laws (local, state and federal) governing your position. Get to know the people and positions relevant to your correctional position and site. (Review Chapter 7 for positions and titles.)

◎ **Starting in-service training (corrections officer or probation/parole), you're *told* new "truths":**

☯ By sheer numbers, the inmates run the institutions...and pre- or post-release: it's management by consent of the governed.

💣 You'll be frequently "tested" by veteran inmates to see whether you'll respond equitably, evenly or grant favors to a chosen few.

☒ You get your days off and holidays based on seniority and, rookie, you're the lowest on the career ladder.

♫ Excess fraternization between employees and inmates is frowned upon.

175.

☪ Supervisors are there to help you get socialized into the correctional system. However, the supervisor must also scrutinize the employee and be wary of substance abuse by the officer and importation (smuggling) of drugs into the correctional facility by the officer for the inmate.

☪ **Changes in attitude and language:** starting to adopt the new organizational culture, resulting in a barrier between you and your friends form your "old life". **For example:** "What's the SOP on a CO responding to an AKA from ODRC's APA?" **Translation:** "What's the standard operating procedure on a corrections officer responding to an also-known-as (alias request) from Ohio Department of Rehabilitation and Corrections' Adult Parole Authority?"

2) **PROBATION:** Usually the first year (for both private and public sector) and includes in-service training period. Did you choose the right career--and right organization?

☪ **Changes in attitude, language, relationship barriers continue.**

☑ **Change in attitude toward inmates, whether a CO or PO.** (CO means Corrections Officer and PO means Probation or Parole Officer, depending on the context.) Effective correctional professionals learn early that the words "offender" and "inmate" do not mean "stupid". Offenders or inmates can be bright, articulate, with a greater intellectual capacity than those paid to manage them. Avoid exhibiting "official arrogance": do *not* be condescending. *But,* remember what veteran corrections professionals have been heard to remark: "Why do you think they (offenders) are referred to as 'Cons'?"

3) **MIDDLE STAGE:** You know what to do, think and feel. You are well-trained and informed; alert and aware; vigilant without being paranoid; constant in the performance of your duties; loyal to peers without being exclusionary; consistent in the treatment--and discipline--of inmates/offenders. You have taken advantage of tuition reimbursement to be eligible--and pass--a promotional exam and may have even been promoted.

◎ **You've *learned* new "truths":**

☺ "...(S)lightly more than 5 percent (of Americans) will be confined in a state or federal prison during their lifetimes" (Gaines, L. K., Kaune, M., & Miller, R. L., 2001, p. 337).

☑ "Over 60 percent of inmates failed to earn a high school diploma" (Gaines, L. K., Kaune, M., & Miller, R. L., 2001, p. 338). This still doesn't make them automatically "stupid", but they are uneducated.

☪ "...(I)nmates are increasingly likely to have been convicted on drug charges and less likely to have been convicted of a violent or property crime" (Gaines, L. K., Kaune, M., & Miller, R. L., 2001, p. 338).

176.

☺ **You combat stressors and stereotypes by being professional on- and off-duty!**

4) **LATER STAGE:** Nearing the end of your *professional* life, you may or may not have seen a promotion take place. Behavioral, attitudinal and lifestyle changes are probably permanent. Good health may persist, but you react at a slower pace. Now, what do you do? Still work hard, become a "short-timer" and just "do your time"? **Above all, have you *planned* (financially, psychologically, and behaviorally) for a post-career life?**

THE INMATE SUBCULTURE

There seems to be a difference of opinion about the inmate subculture, otherwise known as the "inmate code". Our Ohio-based correctional peers in facilities and institutions believe it exists. But, Gaines, L. K., Kaune, M., & Miller, R. L.(2001, p. 339) state: "There has been an influx of youthful inmates and drug offenders who are seen as being only 'out for themselves' and unwilling to follow any code that preaches collective values…the prison code has been replaced by one…of gang loyalties…." **In case you work with inmates (incarcerated, pre- or post-release) who believe in the "inmate code", here's a synopsis of the key factors:**

CODE FACTOR	EXAMPLES
1. RELIABILITY	➤ Don't "snitch" on each other. ➤ Protect the race, culture or gang (now called "security threat groups"). ➤ Inmates do not talk about their crimes.
2. TOUGHNESS	☞ #1 Rule: Each inmate "does his own time", doesn't complain to excess. ☞ Mind your own business.
3. SOCIAL STRUCTURE TO AVOID CONFLICT WITH EACH OTHER	◎ "Pecking order" with sex offenders at the bottom. ◎ Do not interfere with another's opportunity for parole or release. ◎ Punish another who acts inappropriately i.e. take sexual advantage of an inmate in a current relationship.

THE DEPRIVATION MODEL

Gaines, L. K., Kaune, M., & Miller, R. L. (2001, p. 340) state: "(t)he deprivation model can be used to explain the high level of prison violence...the stressful and oppressive conditions of prison life lead to aggressive behavior on the part of the inmates." But, what does this model mean to *you*? Invariably, the inmates will try and corrupt, threaten or force the corrections officer to provide the missing item; thereby helping the inmate to overcome the "pain" of being "deprived" as a result of his or her imprisonment. **How would *you* react in these situation?**

DEPRIVATION (MISSING ITEM)	EXAMPLES OF INMATE COPING STRATEGIES	HOW WOULD YOU REACT?
1. LIBERTY	*Try to run errands. *Ask you to get them a "visitor" for visiting hours. *Try to get furloughs.	
2. GOODS & SERVICES	*Ask you to smuggle in missing tobacco, drugs, food, alcohol, money. *Create "token economy": barter for missing goods and services.	
3. HETERO-SEXUAL RELATIONS	*Ask someone to be a lover. *Create a loving relationship. *Rape another inmate as a substitute for a lover.	
4. AUTONOMY (ability to make your own decisions)	*Ask for (or demand) extra phone call or additional "phone time". *Refuse harmless order from you, "just because they can".	
5. SECURITY	*Ask for isolation/segregation. *Break rules to force you to give them segregation.	

(Adapted from Sykes' 1958 study as quoted by McCarthy, B. J., 2002, p. 260).

CAREER EXPECTATIONS VS. CAREER REALITIES

Again, let me re-iterate. We honestly don't want to be "spoil sports" by saying you can't obtain your dream job and find a career which meets--and exceeds--your expectations. We wish you all the best, really.

But, we also don't want you to experience any stress, frustration or disillusionment because we didn't do *our* job and ask *you* to evaluate your career plan. Therefore, whether you're interested in private- or public-sector corrections, institutional corrections, pre- or post-release, let's temper your enthusiasm with a gentle dose of reality. In other words, **answer the following true/false questions:**

_____ 1. I expect to become an accepted team-player.

_____ 2. I expect to have a supportive supervisor.

_____ 3. My college experience can only help me in this field.

_____ 4. I expect to work with current- and ex-inmates of one race.

_____ 5. I want to work with younger offenders and help them turn their lives around.

_____ 6. I understand prisons are pretty safe: there's really very little violence.

_____ 7. At least I won't have to worry about inmates hurting other inmates: it's against the "inmate code".

_____ 8. Disciplining inmates doesn't have dangerous consequences.

_____ 9. With my skills, knowledge and abilities, I don't anticipate any problem in being promoted.

_____ 10. I know where I will work and expect to be there until retirement.

Well, how did you do on the "Career Expectations vs. Career Realities" quiz? (HINT: The more "true" answers, the more optimistic and, perhaps, unrealistic you are.) Read the next page for more details.

179.

Long version of why you need to temper your enthusiasm with reality:

1. **I expect to become an accepted team-player.** Regrettably, it's inevitable that not everyone will "accept" you...either as an individual or a team-player.

2. **I expect to have a supportive supervisor.** Just checking if you were listening. We already warned you that the supervisor will have the responsibility to socialize you into your new correctional career. But, the supervisor will also be closely scrutinizing your activities, relationships and conversations to ensure you are not being corrupted and/or performing illegal activities.

3. **My college experience can only help me in this field.** We certainly hope so, or our professorial tenure would be in jeopardy. But, sadly, as in the case of your law enforcement, executive-branch brethren, there's the possibility that the "old school" veterans will be threatened by your existence: your age, enthusiasm, dedication to your career and the field could be threatening to their status quo. So, be careful who you choose to emulate and with whom you associate.

4. **I expect to work with current- and ex-inmates of one race.** According to Gaines, L. K., Kaune, M., & Miller, R. L. (2001, p. 337), "...nearly 30 percent of African American males and 16 percent of Hispanic males will be imprisoned at one point in their lives."

5. **I want to work with younger offenders and help them turn their lives around.** Trick question! Again, per Gaines, L. K., Kaune, M., & Miller, R. L.: "...(P)ersons aged eighteen to twenty-four account for the highest percentage of new admissions to prison, approximately 30 percent. The median...is twenty-nine...(though) inmates over the age of fifty will comprise 33 percent of the total prison population by 2010 (versus 10 percent, currently)".

6. **I understand prisons are pretty safe: there's really very little violence.** No, "...prison is a dangerous place to live...the prison culture is predicated on violence...(and) prisoners (use) violence...to establish power and dominance" (Gaines, L. K., Kaune, M., & Miller, R. L., 2001, p. 339).

7. **At least I won't have to worry about inmates hurting other inmates: it's against the "inmate code".** *False!* Read the answer to question #6. Besides, Gaines, L. K., Kaune, M., & Miller, R. L (2001, p. 340) state: "About 100 inmates are murdered by fellow inmates each year, and about 26,000 inmate-on-inmate assaults take place annually."

8. **Disciplining inmates doesn't have dangerous consequences.** *False:* "...criminologists...have noted that collective violence (riots) occurs in response to heightened measures of security at corrections facilities. Thus, the violence

occurs in response to an additional reduction in freedom for inmates" (Gaines, L. K., Kaune, M., & Miller, R. L, 2001, p. 340).

9. **With my skills, knowledge and abilities, I don't anticipate any problem in being promoted.** In the case of correctional officers, promotions are tied to availability, resources, civil service examinations and educational-level achieved. Your probability of being promoted is greater if you have a solid post-secondary education behind you: but, sadly, the promotion is not guaranteed.

10. **I know where I will work and expect to be there until retirement.** As noted in Chapter 13, we hope you're right. But, there are plenty of unforeseen--and unplanned--circumstances which could alter this statement, including organizational consolidations and layoffs, familial and financial obligations, work-related injuries or disabilities and, ultimately, choosing of a new career direction. Again, we wish you all the luck in finding your dream job and a career which meets--even exceeds--your expectations and hope you do not encounter any of these life-altering situations.

FINAL SELF-ASSESSMENT

In Chapter 9, you designed your career plan to achieve your choice of occupations. However, after having just completed the present chapter, how do you evaluate your career expectations against the realities of the private- or public-sector corrections field? **You can find out by answering the following questions:**

1) **What changes in your life can you expect?**

    a. Personal Changes:_____

    _____

    b. Financial Changes:_____

    _____

    c. Relationship Changes:_____

_____

d. Professional Changes:_____

_____

e. Lifestyle Changes:_____

_____

2)   **Prioritize these changes, according to their importance to *your* career plan:**

#1 Priority:_____

#2 Priority:_____

#3 Priority:_____

#4 Priority:_____

#5 Priority:_____

3)   **Assess the likelihood these priorities (changes) will occur:**

PRIORITY/CHANGE	NOT LIKELY TO OCCUR	LIKELY TO OCCUR	VERY LIKELY
#1:			
#2:			
#3:			
#4:			
#5:			

4)   **Using the results from Question #3, re-assess your priority list:**

#1 Priority:_____

#2 Priority:_____

#3 Priority:_____

#4 Priority:_____

#5 Priority:_____

5)   Changes and priorities can only occur if a conscious choice and effort is
made. Do you *want* to make these changes in priorities?

PRIORITY/CHANGE	DO YOU WANT TO DO THIS?	WHAT DO YOU DO NOW?
#1:		
#2:		
#3:		
#4:		
#5:		

CONCLUSION

Several final thoughts. In case you haven't noticed the tone of this chapter, the
corrections officer becomes the "other inmate", subject to daily imprisonment,
deprivations of liberty, under constant temptation and corrupting influences of the inmates
who have time and not much else to do. Corrections professional (corrections *and*
probation and parole officers) must be on guard: both personally and psychologically.
After all, corrections professionals do not have the luxury of their executive branch
brethren, the police: police contacts with "bad people" are brief and short-lived.
Correctional employees must deal with the offender day-in and day-out: the employee
may know the offender's life story; but, the offender also knows the employee's. Special
care should be taken not to become *unduly* supportive of an offender. Keep in mind that
77 percent of all state and federal correctional inmates receive parole or probation
(Gaines, L. K., Kaune, M., & Miller, R. L., 2001, p.350).

But, this workbook is about *you*. Did we diminished *your* interest and enthusiasm for a career in the private- or public-sector, correctional field? How does your Chapter 9 career plan balance against career expectations and career realities resulting from your self-assessment activities in this chapter? Have you planned appropriately, made the commitment of time, effort, resources and longevity necessary to succeed in this field? ***In your sincere and final assessment, do you have what it takes to make this field your career choice?***

SUGGESTED READING

ANY WEBSITE OR BOOK RELATING TO A HOBBY, SPORT, LEISURE ACTIVITY WHICH CATCH YOUR INTEREST!

American Society of Association Executives (over 6,000 associations) at http://info. asaenet.org/gateway/OnlineAssocSList.html

Directory of Associations (over 2,500 associations) at http://www.marketingsource. com/associations

Encyclopedia of Associations, check your local library for this book which includes over 23,000 national and international associations.

National Trade and Professional Associations Directory, available at your local library, it includes"…about 7,600 trade associations, professional societies, labor unions, and technical organizations" (McClelland, 2001, p. 227).

REFERENCES

Gaines, L. K., Kaune, M., & Miller, R. L. (2001). *Criminal justice in action: The core.* Belmont, CA: Wadsworth.

McCarthy, B. J. (2002). Keeping an eye on the keeper: Prison corruption and its control. In Braswell, M. C., McCarthy, B. R. & McCarthy, B. J., *Justice, crime and ethics* (pp. 253-265). Cincinnati, OH: Anderson Publishing Co.

McClelland, C. L. (2001). *Changing careers for dummies.* New York, NY: Hungry Minds, Inc.

A FINAL WORD OF ADVICE FROM YOUR AUTHORS....

Great advice has been dispensed by very wise people. So, we'll let our final words of advice speak through them:

When handling "difficult" people: *"I praise loudly; I blame softly."*
-Catherine II of Russia

When considering salary offers: *"There is a myth that if you amass enough wealth, then your life falls into place.*
-Helen Hunt

When you're getting anxious: *"Having it all doesn't necessarily mean having it all at once."*
-Stephanie Luetkehans

AND, FINALLY: *"There is no scientific answer for success. You can't define it. You've simply got to live it and do it."*
-Anita Roddick